# Murder
## AT THE
# Millpond

Published by Collins
An imprint of HarperCollinsPublishers
Westerhill Road
Bishopbriggs
Glasgow G64 2QT
www.harpercollins.co.uk

HarperCollinsPublishers
Macken House, 39/40 Mayor Street Upper, Dublin 1, D01 C9W8, Ireland

All puzzles supplied by Clarity Media Ltd

First published in 2024
© HarperCollins Publishers 2024

ISBN 978-0-00-871007-1

10 9 8 7 6 5 4

The contents of this publication are believed correct at the time of printing.
Nevertheless the publisher can accept no responsibility for errors or omissions,
changes in the detail given or for any expense or loss thereby caused.

A catalogue record for this book is available from the British Library.

Printed and bound in the UK using 100% renewable electricity at CPI Group
(UK) Ltd

If you would like to comment on any aspect of this book, please contact us at
the given address or online. E-mail: puzzles@harpercollins.co.uk

This book contains FSC™ certified paper and other controlled
sources to ensure responsible forest management.

For more information visit: www.harpercollins.co.uk/green

Collins

MURDER
MYSTERY
PUZZLES

# Murder
## AT THE
# Millpond

**100** COSY CRIME PUZZLES

# INTRODUCTION

"A little slice of heaven located in the English countryside."
That was how the estate agent had described Ivyville and the
neighbouring village of Upper Gorsetown to Detective Heather
Vintner as she toured picturesque properties in the vicinity. Such
a description would hardly seem accurate now.

Nowhere, no matter how tranquil or how genteel, is immune
to Death and his nefarious clutches. Cold-blooded murder,
however, is quite another thing. Little did Heather know that,
as the ink was drying on her newly-signed lease, two residents of
Upper Gorsetown were enjoying their last sunrises and supping
their last suppers. But such is life and, you might say, such is
death.

After the initial shock, the questions are legion. "How could
something so horrible happen in a place as lovely as this?" is a
common one, regurgitated in endless newspaper articles that
contrast the beauty of the location with the stark reality of what
has happened. In the aftermath of such an event, community
leaders duly give reassuring platitudes and politicians look
earnestly and plaintively at the cameras and make all the right
noises.

The harder job goes to those like Detective Vintner. She must ask
why anyone would want to commit such a crime and, crucially,
*who* would want to. This is her story as she pursues justice in her
own inimitable style. Heather knows that murder is murder, no
matter how bucolic the setting.

Solve along with Heather as details of the crime are unveiled, the main suspects are introduced, and the investigation duly unfolds to its conclusion as the case is finally cracked. I recommend that you solve in order from puzzle one to 100 as the story is intertwined with the puzzles, and at times later puzzles reveal the answers to earlier ones. It is therefore best to start your puzzling journey at the beginning and end at the end.

This book includes a large array of puzzles that will test all your detective skills, and features a range of logic, word, visual and numerical puzzles. Some will be quick to solve whilst others will be decidedly chewy. If you ever get completely stuck, or simply want to check your problem-solving skills haven't led you astray, full solutions can be found at the back of the book on pages 211-241. In this section, you will also find some useful keys for deciphering codes, on pages 242-244.

Welcome to Upper Gorsetown. I do hope you enjoy your visit. Murder notwithstanding.

Happy sleuthing!

Dan Moore

# PUZZLES

#  BODY SEARCH

Detective Heather Vintner is enjoying a leisurely breakfast at her home, a peaceful cottage in Ivyville, a small countryside hamlet. Her phone rings just as she is about to dip her fried bread into her runny egg. "Typical!" she thinks to herself. A phone call at this exact second is about as welcome as rain at a barbecue. It's her work phone, so she decides she best answer the call. Although she's been a detective for a few years it's her first month in a new job, and she wants to make a good impression.

"What's that you say? A murder? At the millpond? I'll be right there…"

Minutes later, Heather is driving through the narrow lanes of nearby Upper Gorsetown, a sizeable village containing around a thousand residents at the last census. She finds herself rushing past the picturesque village green and church before arriving at the millpond that apparently used to provide the water for a long defunct watermill. The millpond is located in a forest clearing, and the surrounding area is popular with dog walkers, ramblers and local foragers.

Heather arrives and is met by flashing blue lights and a stern-looking colleague who ushers her to the body which has been found by a walker near the millpond.

Locate the position of the body in the diagram shown. Each square represents a single pace. The body is located five paces away from the nearest tree and six paces away from the other two trees, by the most direct route moving horizontally or vertically from square to square.

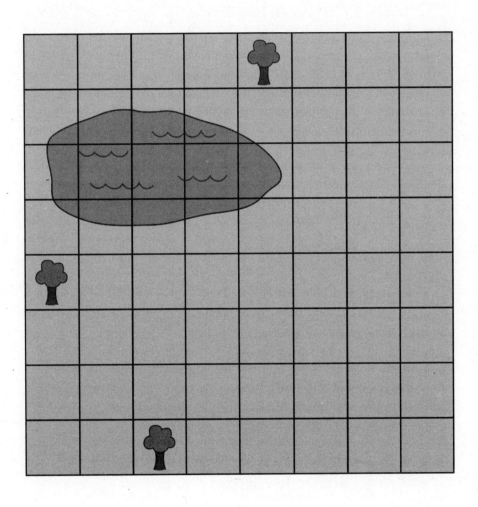

#  KNIFE CRIME

Having reached the body, Heather lets out an audible gasp. It's immediately evident that the poor soul has been stabbed. Having read about typical crimes in the area before taking the job, Heather is pretty sure she's seen no mention of violent crimes such as this. From what she can tell, crimes in Upper Gorsetown and the surrounding area normally amount to little more than a child stealing some sweets from the corner shop when the owner isn't looking. Life is normally sedate and relatively simple around these parts. But murder – that doesn't belong to an idyllic village like this.

Heather knows she won't be back home and finishing off her breakfast any time soon – this is serious. Examining the location of the wound, she duly records the details of the crime in her notebook as various forensics officers mill around, putting a cordon of police tape around the area to protect the crime scene and keep nosy villagers (which is most of them) at bay.

Solve this word puzzle to deduce where on the body the victim had been stabbed. A tick in a box indicates a letter appears in the word in the same position, whilst arrows indicate the letter appears in the word, but in a different position. If a square is blank, the letter does not appear in the word. The word consists of five different letters.

| P | I | O | U | S |
| C | L | Á | N | K |
| ⟷T | ⟷R | Ă | M | S |
| ⟷R | É | Á | L | M |

**ANSWER**

| | | | | |

# SILENT WITNESS

A nasty business indeed. Baffled by what has led to this gruesome fate, Heather decides to speak to the person who found the body, Jeremy Johnston, who she is informed is a keen local rambler. At first he seems so shocked he is unable to speak and just stares at Heather with a bewildered expression on his face. She sits him down and asks him to take a deep breath. After a couple of minutes, he has calmed down sufficiently to start talking:

"7:57am, it was. That time will be seared on my brain for as long as I'm alive. I was on my morning stroll when suddenly I came across the body, just lying there on the grass. It's enough to make me want a stiff brandy, let me tell you, and I'm not much of a drinker. Of course what makes it worse is that I know him. It's… oh, no, I don't think I can bring myself to say it."

Mr. Johnston writes the name down on a piece of paper for Heather, however his hands are still visibly shaking from the shock of it all, and what he writes down looks very strange indeed. Can you reconstruct the victim's name?

DE JI IJ PA KEL

L TN NIS DAI R

#  OPEN TO DISPUTE

Heather thanks him for the name, and then asks when he last saw Dennis Baker alive.

"I'm not entirely sure as I'm very bad at keeping track of time – if I had to hazard a guess I'd say a couple of days ago, just a friendly nod as we walked past each other in the street. Though I did hear he had a bit of an argument with someone last night."

Her interest piqued by this potential lead for investigation, Heather asks him to elaborate.

"I wasn't there, but I heard through the grapevine he had something of an altercation with Sam Turner at the pub yesterday afternoon. Of course, they're both members of the local foraging society. I'm told there was also a lady present, but I don't know who that was. Ask Gus who's the pub landlord, he's something of a pillar of the local community, everyone knows and likes him."

Mr. Johnston is clearly very upset, and Heather decides it is best not to question him any further for now.

Solve this codeword to find out what members of the Upper Gorsetown society forage for. Each number from 1–26 represents a letter of the alphabet from A–Z. Every letter appears in the grid at least once, and is represented by just one number. For instance, 11 stands for the letter A. Crack the entire code to complete the crossword grid.

| | | | | | | | | | | | | |
|---|---|---|---|---|---|---|---|---|---|---|---|---|
| 6 | 17 | 1 | 4 | 2 | 16 | 6 | 5 | ■ | 10 | 6 | 22 | 1 |
| 19 | ■ | 6 | ■ | 6 | ■ | 20 | ■ | 21 | ■ | 17 | ■ | 13 |
| 1 | 22 | 11 | 23 | 20 | ■ | 8 | ■ | 13 | 19 | 10 | 6 | 2 |
| 15 | ■ | 7 | ■ | 13 | ■ | 23 | ■ | 6 | ■ | 23 | ■ | 8 |
| ■ | ■ | 13 | 20 | 18 | 6 | 11 | 19 | 23 | 14 | 22 | 6 | 6 |
| 24 | ■ | 18 | ■ | 24 | ■ | 5 | ■ | 16 | ■ | 23 | ■ | 15 |
| 4 | 2 | 23 | 3 | 23 | 20 | ■ | 14 | 23 | 19 | 16 | 2 | 4 |
| 20 | ■ | 20 | ■ | 11 | ■ | 11 | ■ | 4 | ■ | 19 | ■ | 2 |
| 19 | 25 | 11 | 16 | 16 | 6 | 2 | 23 | 20 | 3 | ■ | ■ | ■ |
| 13 | ■ | 20 | ■ | 23 | ■ | 25 | ■ | 11 | ■ | 9 | ■ | 13 |
| 25 | 23 | 24 | 2 | 4 | ■ | 11 | ■ | 14 | 22 | 4 | 12 | 19 |
| 6 | ■ | 6 | ■ | 20 | ■ | 5 | ■ | 22 | ■ | 22 | ■ | 6 |
| 2 | 6 | 5 | 4 | ■ | 3 | 11 | 26 | 6 | 16 | 16 | 6 | 19 |

A B C D E F G H I J K L M N O P Q R S T U V W X Y Z

| 1 | 2 | 3 | 4 | 5 | 6 | 7 | 8 | 9 | 10 | 11 A | 12 | 13 |
|---|---|---|---|---|---|---|---|---|---|---|---|---|

| 14 | 15 Y | 16 | 17 | 18 | 19 | 20 N | 21 | 22 | 23 | 24 | 25 | 26 |
|---|---|---|---|---|---|---|---|---|---|---|---|---|

| 25 | 13 | 19 | 10 | 2 | 4 | 4 | 25 | 19 |
|---|---|---|---|---|---|---|---|---|

# 5     HOME VISIT

Heather takes stock. She knows that Dennis Baker has been stabbed to death, and that Jeremy Johnston found the body. She has also found out that he argued with Sam Turner, a fellow forager, together with someone else the day before he died. Her obvious next port of call is Sam Turner's house – she needs to find out what the argument was about, and whether it was serious enough for Sam to be considered a murder suspect.

Heather hops in her car and drives to Privet Lane, where Sam Turner lives. It seems a bit incongruous to be thinking about a gruesome murder as she scoots past hedgerows bursting with flower and listens to the mellifluous song of a lapwing as it flies up in the air in such a carefree manner from one of the nearby fields. A farmer is toiling away nearby, and life goes on as normal for the vast majority of Upper Gorsetown residents whilst one of their number is no longer of this world. Such is life.

It doesn't take her long to reach Mr. Turner's house and, as she rings the doorbell, she does so with a little trepidation as to what she will discover: might she even see the murder weapon or perhaps bloodstained clothing? Or, perhaps more plausibly, she might hear the background hum of a washing machine working away to try and remove blood stains from clothing – she'd heard from someone in forensics they are a bit of a nightmare to wash out.

Use the clues to work out Sam's house number:

— The Newton family live two doors up from the Turner family.

— The Giles family live one door up from the Thatchers.

— The Newtons and the Crumpets are neighbours.

— The Presleys live two doors down from the Crumpets.

— The Newtons are located two doors down from the Giles family.

UP

DOWN

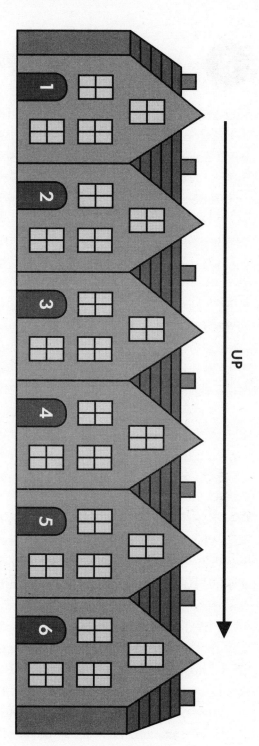

#  KNOCK, KNOCK

Her heart beating a little quicker than usual, Heather knocks at the door. She tries to keep an open mind; years of detective work have led her to never assume anything, at least as much as humanly possible. As unnerving as it is, she also feels alive at moments like this: it beats sitting in a car for hours on end munching on soggy sandwiches from the local shop whilst waiting for something, anything of interest to happen. Life here seemed a lot more sedate than in the big city – until now.

After a brief pause, the door slowly creaks open, and Heather is greeted by a pale-looking woman who has clearly been crying.

"Oh hello, my dear, are you here to ask me some questions about Sam's death?"

Heather does a double-take. This is not how she thought the conversation would go! Flustered, all she can muster is an "Erm… can you tell me what happened?"

"I'm Sam's wife, Sandy. Sam had been out picking mushrooms yesterday, and then apparently felt very sick in the evening. I'd been out until late, you see, and when I got home he staggered around babbling incoherently for a minute and then immediately collapsed, so I called 999 and had him rushed to hospital. Very sadly he died overnight. I've just come back to get a few things and make a couple of calls to relatives then I'm going straight back to the hospital. Well, I'm assuming he accidentally picked the wrong mushrooms, but I don't know, I just don't know, he was so experienced…" With that, her words trail off and she breaks down in tears, and Heather finds herself in the strange position of hugging the wife of the man who was her prime suspect.

Picking mushrooms is a dangerous business. A delicious meal and a deadly one can sometimes only be separated by small differences between mushrooms that look similar but have very disparate effects on the body. Put your ability to spot subtle differences to the test. Look at the two groups of mushrooms here – can you circle the five differences in the bottom image and deduce whether the mushrooms are safe to eat or not?

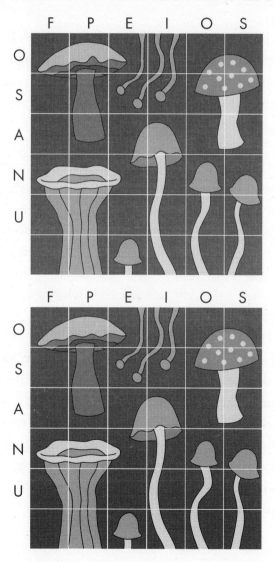

# IS IT ALL AN ACT?

Heather shudders as the thought occurs to her that she might be hugging a double-murderer. Could Sandy have killed Dennis and her own husband? If true, then she was the best actress in the world, worthy of an Oscar, as standing before her is what appears to be a truly distraught woman.

"When did I become so cynical?" Heather thinks to herself. She has seen enough documentaries where a distraught relative making public appeals for information on the disappearance of a loved one turns out to be the killer all along. It's a cliché because it's true: appearances can be deceptive.

She delicately asks Sandy a few more questions, aware that she does not want the grieving widow to feel like a suspect, at least not unless she has good reason to suspect her. Sandy says she had been at a friend's house most of the day before returning home to find Sam in a terrible state – something that Heather would of course check was true – and she had no idea that Sam had been at the pub earlier in the day, nor any idea who he could have been arguing with.

Satisfied that she should take Sandy at face value, Heather says goodbye. As she's leaving she ponders the fact that there hadn't been a murder in the Gorsetown area for years and now there were potentially two at once, if a link between the two deaths could be proved. Were murders like buses around here? And was this a good time to have joined the local force or a bad one? Heather decides it depends on whether she manages to solve the case successfully or not!

She heads to the pub to see if she can find out more information about the argument that apparently took place between the two dead men and an unknown third party.

Solve this riddle to reveal the name of the pub:

*My first is in country and in cow,*
*My second is in horse but not in plough,*
*My third is in orchard but not in pear,*
*My fourth is not in bull but is in beware,*
*My fifth is in run but not in hare.*

# 8 LOCAL KNOWLEDGE

The pub is the beating heart of the local community, at least according to the sign in its entrance. Heather goes inside The Crown and the familiar pub scent of stale beer and salt and vinegar crisps hits her, strangely triggering some happy memories of good times in her local pub back home in her formative years. "Focus, Heather," she says to herself. On surveying the scene, she sees what she imagines to be the usual suspects, people who prop up the bar and hence the pub's sales day in, day out. It must be hard running a pub, she muses, as owners have to manage their customers' sobriety but at the same time also manage their bottom line.

The owner, Gus Hawkins, is nowhere to be seen. She asks at the bar where she can find him, but not before ordering a drink: it's only right to support the local community, after all. Sipping on her lime and soda, the cheapest drink she could think of, she looks at the strange note that she has been slipped by the barman.

"Sorry to be so cryptic about it," says the barman, "but Gus doesn't like to be interrupted when he's not serving front of house, so he ensures if someone asks for him they have something important to discuss by challenging them to solve a puzzle first. If they don't bother, then he knows it can't be important. Gus is so popular around these parts that otherwise he'd never get a minute to himself. I'm sure you understand."

Where should Heather go to find the owner?

THE CROWN

# THE PLOT *THICKENS*... SOMEHOW (8)

# 9 COOKING UP A STORM

Heather goes through to the kitchens and finds Gus Hawkins deep in conversation with the chef. He abruptly stops talking and smiles at her uneasily, frowning in the process whilst trying to decide if he recognises her or not.

"Afternoon, Gus. How are you doing today? I'm Detective Heather Vintner, and I'm here to ask you whether you noticed anything strange in the pub yesterday."

Gus is initially evasive, and says nothing immediately comes to mind. Heather lets him know it was a leading question and she is already aware of there being something of an altercation the previous day between Dennis Baker and Sam Turner.

"Sorry for being a little coy, detective," says Gus. "It's just that death, well, it's bad for business you know… people come in for a burger and a pint, they don't want to think they could be dead a few hours later!" Heather gives a little nod of acknowledgement – he has clearly heard about the death of Dennis Baker – news travels fast in these parts, evidently.  She lets him know that it's worse than that – both Dennis and Sam Turner are dead.

"Dear me, dear me," mutters Gus, "I was aware of hearing raised voices, but it's my business to keep out of other people's business, if you know what I mean. But both of them dead? What is the world coming to?" He shakes his head in disbelief.

Heather mentions she has heard there was a third person involved, and Gus says he can't recall in detail but certainly if there was he didn't recognise them. He says that Dennis and Sam were good friends with each other, though it wouldn't be unusual for them to argue as they were both very opinionated. They also both knew Jeremy Johnston quite well, though Gus suspects the latter was a little jealous of them as he lived in their shadow to some degree.

Heather's ears prick up at the mention of Jeremy Johnston – should he be considered a suspect, not just the person who unfortunately stumbled across the body of Dennis? He was in no state to talk to her in detail earlier, so she resolves to go and see him again shortly once the initial shock has worn off. She asks Gus if there is any CCTV footage she can look at from the day before, but he informs her that the system isn't working at the moment. Heather wonders if any CCTV system does actually work anywhere in the country – if she had a penny for every time one didn't work when she'd needed the footage, she'd be rich!

Suddenly Heather's stomach rumbles, and she realises she never had time to eat her breakfast. Gus perks up in an instant, reminding Heather of how a baby can go from bawling its eyes out to giggling hysterically within mere seconds. Gus is evidently never one to miss an opportunity for some business and passes Heather the menu. Her head slightly scrambled from all she has been through this morning, Heather struggles to make sense of the menu – can you unscramble the letters to reveal the five main courses available on the lunch menu?

# THE CROWN
# MENU

---

### FINCH HID PASS (4, 3, 5)

### BRASH NAGS NAMED (7, 3, 4)

### ALE SANG (7)

### HOST ROOM TOURISM (8, 7)

### POETIC GATE (7, 3)

---

# ⑩ BUILDING BRIDGES

Funnily enough Heather decides to avoid the mushroom risotto and tucks into some battered cod with proper chunky chips, the ones that can handle a good dousing with vinegar without going limp and soggy. As her dad would say, "You can never go wrong with fish and chips." Well, apart from that one time it gave him terrible food poisoning and he was laid up in bed for days, but that's not to be dwelt on.

After her meal, Heather drives to see Jeremy Johnston. She finds him at home, sipping on a brandy, just like he had mentioned when she first spoke to him. He looks calmer than earlier. Deciding that honesty is the best policy, Heather informs him that Sam Turner is also dead. Jeremy breaks down and tells Heather that he is – *was* – good friends with Sam and indeed Dennis. He starts shaking and getting very upset as he processes the news and Heather realises she made the wrong call – he's in no state for her to ask him the tough questions now.

Heather therefore asks Jeremy what he thinks the argument between the two dead men in the pub could have been about. He insists he has no idea, and goes on to explain that the three of them were childhood friends who attended the local school, Saint Patrick's, together. Sam and Dennis had even gone to university together, and were generally as thick as thieves. Apart from being overly competitive for Jeremy's liking, they were people he liked very much. Jeremy was in awe of their ability to tell edible mushrooms from deadly ones that looked scarily similar.

Heather thinks that it sounds like there wasn't *mushroom* for disagreement between the two men, then mentally scolds herself for joking about it when they have lost their lives – decorum, and all that.

Heather asks if Jeremy is aware of anyone that either of the dead men could have made enemies of. Jeremy says no-one immediately comes to mind. He then proceeds to give her the names of some other people who attend the foraging society meetings that the three of them have been members of for a while. He says that things can get heated and turn into arguments, though Heather can't imagine how. Just as she is about to leave, he says, "Talk to Carol: she knows everything about everyone! I chat to her regularly to find out what's going on around here! She'll be at the village hall." He then proceeds to give her brief details on all the people he mentions, and who gets on with who.

Once she is outside Heather looks at the list of names that Jeremy has provided. She tries to draw connections and links between who knows who, and how, until she has lines going everywhere across her notepad and the whole thing looks like a doodle drawn on an aeroplane experiencing severe turbulence.

Create a more orderly set of links by connecting every island (represented by circles) into a single interconnected group. To do this draw bridges between islands. The number in each circle states how many bridges must be connected to that island. Bridges cannot cross each other, can only be drawn horizontally or vertically, and there can be a maximum of two bridges between any pair of islands.

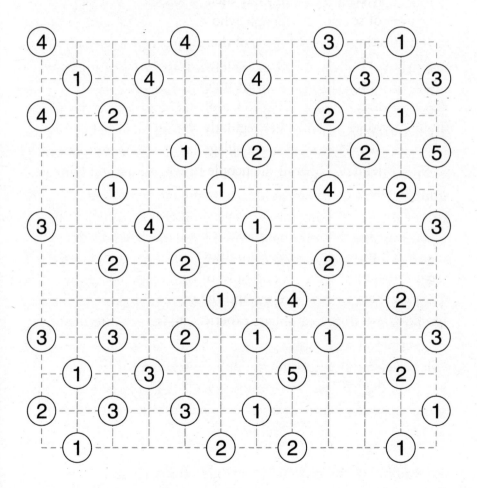

# MUSIC HALL

Heather arrives at the village hall just as it is getting dark. The lights are on inside, and there is a pleasant hum of activity as tables are being rearranged and tablecloths and decorations placed on them. Classical music is playing in the background. Heather introduces herself to the first person she sees, who as luck would have it turns out to be Carol Noel.

As expected, Carol – and no doubt the rest of the room – have now heard about the murders, which at least saves Heather the unpleasant job of having to break the news again.

"It's been the talk of the town, of course! Well, village, but that's not a phrase, is it, dear? And to think I talked to Sam just yesterday about committee business," Carol says with a slight shudder. Heather ushers her into a small empty room filled with dusty files. As she does so, several other people look at her, pausing their activities momentarily, but then they quickly go back to work. Heather closes the door.

"I'm here because Jeremy Johnston mentioned you are the beating heart of the community. Do you know of anyone who had bad blood with either Dennis or Sam?" She is quite pleased with herself for repurposing the pub's entry sign for her own purposes: she has learned over the years that giving people a little ego massage can help coax them into telling you what you want to know.

"Do you know, my dear, now I come to think about it, there was a blazing row between Sam Turner and someone else not so long ago at one of our meetings. I'm the secretary of the society, you see, so I tend to know what's going on. Not that I'm one for gossip, mind." In Heather's experience, whenever people say that it really means that they love gossiping. Just like when someone repeatedly says something doesn't bother them, it's a surefire thing that it *really* annoys them.

Solve this puzzle to discover the name of the person who rowed with Sam. You must enter each letter from A-Z into the grid once to fill the crossword grid. The numbered letters will reveal the name.

| S | W | A | 9 | ■ | A | D | 1,7 | U | S | T | 10 | D |
|---|---|---|---|---|---|---|---|---|---|---|---|---|
| T | | D | | | R | | N | | E | | | U |
| R | H | I | | O | M | E | | C | A | | | S |
| I | E | | R | A | | U | M | | | | | |
| C | O | 2 | N | T | E | R | C | L | A | 4 | M | ■ |
| K | | | U | | | T | | N | | | | |
| E | N | J | O | I | N | ■ | I | L | I | E | U | |
| N | | 8 | T | D | | | | | | | E | |
| ■ | E | C | 6 | O | L | O | A | T | I | O | N | |
| | U | U | | | T | N | | | | C | | |
| A | L | E | S | ■ | 11 | 5 | E | A | T | H | | |
| R | A | L | E | D | A | E | | | | | | |
| A | R | N | Y | R | D | ■ | 3 | Y | E | D | | |

A B C D E F G H I J K L M N O P Q R S T U V W X Y Z

| 1 | 2 | 3 | 4 | 5 | 6 | 7 | 8 | 9 | 10 | 11 |
|---|---|---|---|---|---|---|---|---|---|---|
| | | | | | | | | | | |

# 12 A SEAT AT THE TABLE

Heather thanks Carol for the information. "And where can I find this Judith?"

"Right over there," says Carol, pointing at a table in the hall. "I've never trusted her. Fingers in too many pies if you ask me, that one. She's clever, too. She's a big chess and bridge player and she studied philosophy at university. Well there's a fancy degree if ever I heard one. It's of no use in the real world though, and she ended up in finance! Still, it's better than some of the so-called credible subjects people study these days… I read in the paper the other day that you can get a degree in…" Heather feels a rant about the youth of today coming on, something she has no time for, so instead zones out from what Carol is saying and waits for the talking to end so she can go over to Judith.

Eight people are sitting down at a circular table. Solve this logic puzzle to work out at which seat each person is sitting, and therefore identify which of them is Judith.

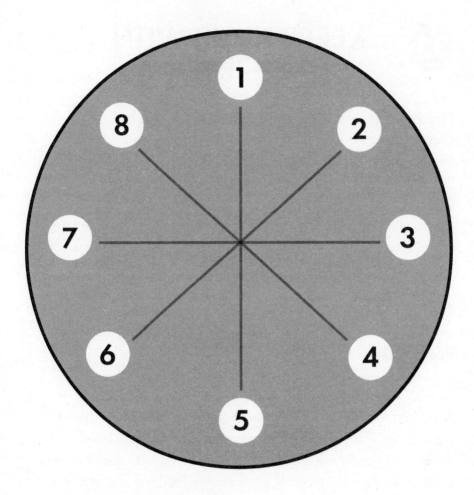

— Zac and Jimi are sitting next to each other.
— Olivia is not in seat 1.
— Frida is opposite Alya.
— Sanjay is in seat 7.
— Lily is not opposite Zac.
— Jimi is opposite Olivia.
— Sanjay is sitting next to Zac.
— Frida is sitting next to Olivia.

Given the lines indicate who is sitting opposite who, where is Judith sitting?

# KEEPING UP WITH THE JONESES

Heather goes over to the table and introduces herself to Judith, then takes her into a corner away from prying eyes and ears. Judith is immediately quite defensive:

"I knew Carol would suggest you talk to me. A right so-and-so, that one, always meddling in other people's business, you know? Never liked her myself. I'm sure you know people like that – annoying, aren't they?"

"Sure, friends like that can be annoying," agrees Heather, "but in my line of work people like that are invaluable," she adds with a light chuckle.

Judith nods, unimpressed, then says: "I'm assuming Carol delighted in telling you that I had a big argument with Sam a week or so ago? It's pathetic really. We used to be an item back in the day, but he always played hot and cold with me. And he's been doing it again recently with society business: the elections are coming up soon for the new committee and Sam had promised me he'd vote for me as secretary if I voted for him to be co-chairman, along with Dennis. Well, that would mean the end of Jeremy as chairman of the society, of course." Heather notes this down – somehow she didn't know Jeremy was currently in charge of the group.

"Anyhow, I found out that he'd promised the exact same thing to Clara Jacobson. Caught them having the exact conversation he'd had with me, so I did. Well, as you can imagine, that didn't sit right with me. Had it out with him there and then! I'll admit to feeling cheated by Sam and it annoyed me to see him being so friendly with Clara, but no, I didn't kill him, thank you very much!"

Heather asks if Jeremy would have known that Sam and Dennis were actively looking to take on the running of the society. "Well, Carol and Jeremy are close, so… it's possible Jeremy knew," said Judith, effectively saying 'yes' in as non-committal a way as possible.

"You know who you should really speak to? Dennis Baker's ex-wife. There was a lot of bad blood between them, and they always snipe at each other whenever they are together now."

Tired after a long day, Heather decides to leave it there for the night. Judith gives her the name of Dennis's ex-wife and resolves to call on her first thing tomorrow. Solve this puzzle to reveal the name. Numbers around the edge of the grid indicate how many consecutive squares to shade in the respective row/column. Commas indicate a gap of at least one blank square between sets of shaded squares. For instance a clue of 4,3 means that somewhere in the region there is a set of four shaded squares, followed by at least one empty square, then another three shaded squares.

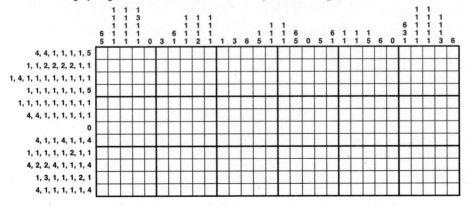

# WHO'S THERE?

The next morning, after a hearty breakfast that Heather allows herself on the basis they are strictly 'compensatory calories' for missing breakfast the day before, she drives over to Gemma Evans' cottage. She makes a mental note that it is fairly close to the millpond.

She knocks on the door twice – knock, knock.

"Who's there?" comes the response. Heather laughs to herself – is this a real life knock, knock joke in the making?

"It's the police," she replies, eschewing the chance to make a terrible joke, which is unlike her, but seems only right in the circumstances.

The door opens, and a girl is standing there looking slightly apprehensive. There is music playing in the background. Heather finds out her name is Layla Baker and that she is Gemma's daughter. Heather asks Layla how old she is. Layla says that her mother is twice her own age. However, six years ago, her mother was 2½ times her age. How old are Layla and Gemma?

# (15) PLAYING GAMES

Heather enters the house and is shown into the living room by Layla. The music grows louder, and it becomes apparent that Gemma is playing the piano. Heather tries to engage her in conversation, but she seems intent on finishing her piece. A couple of minutes later, the piece comes to a dramatic conclusion and Gemma turns around.

"Hello, Gemma," says Heather. "I'm here to ask you some questions about your ex-husband, Dennis Baker."

"I wondered how long it would be before the police turned up!" replies Gemma, before continuing: "Of course I'll answer all your questions, but, no offence, I'd like to check your brain is up to the task first."

"None taken," replies Heather, being very British despite being slightly offended.

"As you can see, officer" – "It's detective, actually," interrupts Heather. She wouldn't normally cut in, but Gemma had got her back up.

"Sorry – *detective*. As you can see, I'm something of a musician. Imagine I play up and down this scale repeatedly – C,D,E,F,G,A,B,C – such that I play C,D,E,F,G,A,B,C,B,A,G,F, E,D,C,D,E,F,G,A,B,C and so forth. Clearly, 'C' is the first note I would play, but what would be the 400th note?" She then adds, somewhat sarcastically, "I'm sure with your detective's mental acuity you will be able to answer in mere seconds." Maths is not Heather's forte, but she wants to win this battle of wits. What is the answer?

# 16 YEARS AND YEARS

Satisfied with the answer, Gemma responds to Heather's questions about Dennis. She acknowledges that her relationship with him had been in difficulty for a while before they eventually went their separate ways.

"And how has your relationship been recently?" Heather probes.

"Oh, not too bad – obviously we share a daughter in Layla so we still have a reasonable amount of contact, and I need things to be civil for her sake. The idea that I'd brood over a divorce that happened years ago and suddenly decide to kill my former husband years later is crazy."

Heather makes a mental note that this doesn't quite match the portrayal of her current relationship with Dennis as portrayed by Judith. "How many years ago did you get divorced, out of interest?" asks Heather.

Solve the puzzle to find out when. Count the number of times the word 'YEAR' appears in this wordsearch grid. The number of times it appears reveals how many years ago Gemma and Dennis got divorced, according to Gemma.

```
Y  A  A  Y  A  A  R  Y  Y  Y
A  E  R  A  Y  E  A  A  Y  Y
E  R  A  R  R  A  Y  Y  Y  Y
A  R  Y  R  A  E  E  E  E  Y
E  Y  A  R  Y  A  E  A  Y  A
E  E  R  R  R  E  E  R  E  A
R  R  E  Y  A  R  R  E  E  E
Y  Y  Y  E  R  A  E  A  E  A
A  A  A  R  R  E  A  Y  E  R
Y  E  A  R  E  Y  R  E  E  Y
```

#  GUT INSTINCT

Gemma's answers seem plausible enough, thinks Heather. But something feels slightly amiss, and she can't put her finger on quite what it is.

She has learned to trust her instinct over the years, as not doing so has cost her from time to time. She thinks of an occasion when she was treated by a dentist who had bad teeth himself and she wanted to walk straight out. "If he can't look after his own teeth, how can he look after mine?" she'd thought at the time. She had stayed through politeness, and then he 'accidentally' knocked out one of her other teeth whilst treating decay in its neighbour. Or that time she followed advice in a book about relationships written by a self-help guru who it transpired had been divorced twice. Acting on the tips had just accelerated the end of the relationship she'd been trying to save. Heather doesn't read self-help books anymore – she figures that if they work then the audience for them should be shrinking, not growing!

After a while Heather realises what has been bugging her about Gemma. Study the grids carefully and shade any differences you find to see what has been puzzling Heather.

| 57 | 42 | 20 | 82 | 77 | 36 | 31 | 19 | 74 | 67 | 19 | 92 | 86 | 75 | 10 |
|----|----|----|----|----|----|----|----|----|----|----|----|----|----|----|
| 51 | 33 | 58 | 79 | 55 | 21 | 59 | 43 | 88 | 5  | 49 | 59 | 68 | 96 | 92 |
| 58 | 18 | 24 | 15 | 12 | 2  | 64 | 30 | 25 | 80 | 17 | 28 | 77 | 45 | 85 |
| 9  | 28 | 65 | 87 | 10 | 24 | 61 | 21 | 89 | 34 | 66 | 19 | 61 | 52 | 1  |
| 61 | 12 | 42 | 63 | 68 | 91 | 18 | 1  | 85 | 43 | 45 | 31 | 91 | 75 | 92 |
| 6  | 4  | 96 | 44 | 86 | 91 | 94 | 74 | 84 | 83 | 33 | 44 | 75 | 46 | 92 |
| 16 | 82 | 7  | 47 | 87 | 88 | 99 | 75 | 9  | 5  | 92 | 60 | 94 | 95 | 84 |
| 78 | 30 | 79 | 67 | 92 | 34 | 81 | 87 | 11 | 19 | 96 | 29 | 57 | 65 | 21 |
| 26 | 87 | 8  | 58 | 29 | 68 | 6  | 43 | 8  | 53 | 56 | 13 | 89 | 90 | 60 |
| 10 | 88 | 97 | 41 | 81 | 93 | 96 | 54 | 55 | 38 | 4  | 76 | 18 | 20 | 93 |
| 41 | 88 | 95 | 74 | 75 | 89 | 14 | 19 | 66 | 3  | 44 | 26 | 28 | 75 | 80 |
| 94 | 73 | 91 | 49 | 92 | 58 | 69 | 71 | 31 | 43 | 85 | 74 | 39 | 60 | 21 |
| 30 | 39 | 74 | 6  | 74 | 61 | 26 | 72 | 52 | 41 | 40 | 59 | 49 | 35 | 71 |
| 73 | 11 | 78 | 75 | 87 | 13 | 2  | 64 | 29 | 8  | 63 | 16 | 75 | 56 | 20 |
| 44 | 88 | 27 | 89 | 10 | 10 | 22 | 70 | 45 | 92 | 6  | 30 | 90 | 51 | 88 |

| 57 | 42 | 20 | 82 | 77 | 36 | 31 | 8  | 74 | 67 | 19 | 92 | 86 | 75 | 10 |
|----|----|----|----|----|----|----|----|----|----|----|----|----|----|----|
| 51 | 33 | 58 | 79 | 55 | 21 | 59 | 43 | 88 | 5  | 49 | 59 | 68 | 96 | 92 |
| 33 | 33 | 84 | 15 | 12 | 2  | 64 | 53 | 25 | 80 | 17 | 28 | 77 | 45 | 85 |
| 38 | 28 | 65 | 87 | 10 | 24 | 61 | 69 | 89 | 34 | 66 | 19 | 61 | 52 | 1  |
| 9  | 12 | 42 | 63 | 68 | 91 | 18 | 97 | 85 | 43 | 45 | 31 | 91 | 75 | 92 |
| 93 | 4  | 96 | 44 | 86 | 91 | 94 | 86 | 84 | 83 | 33 | 44 | 75 | 46 | 92 |
| 16 | 82 | 7  | 47 | 87 | 88 | 99 | 75 | 9  | 5  | 92 | 60 | 94 | 95 | 84 |
| 78 | 89 | 60 | 51 | 92 | 34 | 81 | 87 | 11 | 4  | 37 | 99 | 4  | 65 | 21 |
| 79 | 87 | 8  | 58 | 21 | 68 | 6  | 43 | 8  | 90 | 56 | 13 | 68 | 90 | 60 |
| 5  | 88 | 97 | 41 | 73 | 93 | 96 | 54 | 55 | 41 | 4  | 76 | 3  | 20 | 93 |
| 99 | 88 | 95 | 74 | 53 | 89 | 14 | 19 | 66 | 69 | 98 | 44 | 89 | 75 | 80 |
| 13 | 73 | 91 | 49 | 73 | 58 | 69 | 71 | 31 | 43 | 85 | 74 | 36 | 60 | 21 |
| 30 | 39 | 74 | 6  | 74 | 61 | 26 | 72 | 52 | 41 | 40 | 59 | 25 | 35 | 71 |
| 73 | 11 | 78 | 75 | 87 | 13 | 2  | 64 | 29 | 86 | 88 | 70 | 60 | 56 | 20 |
| 44 | 88 | 27 | 89 | 10 | 10 | 22 | 70 | 45 | 92 | 6  | 30 | 90 | 51 | 88 |

# 18 THAT RINGS A BELL

That's it! Heather thinks it is strange that Gemma is wearing a wedding ring, yet has been divorced for six years! She also notes it is not a great fit, seemingly being a little too large for Gemma's finger. Gemma is a slender woman, so perhaps she has just lost weight since she first married.

"Have you remarried, Gemma?" she asks.

"No – no I haven't!" She looks down at the ring on her finger and realises why Heather has asked. "Oh that," she chuckles. "Old habits die hard, don't they?" She realises it's not a very credible response, but she doesn't want to tell Heather the real reason.

Heather gives a slight smile. She is not convinced, although she's never been married so maybe she's missing something. She would say the phrase 'always the bridesmaid and never the bride' applies to her, except she's never actually been a bridesmaid either.

Heather asks Gemma for her contact details so she can get in touch if she needs to, and she duly hands over her business card. It transpires she works for a tech company. Heather sees Gemma's email and phone number are on the back of the card, but she is intrigued by the logo on the front of the card. Can you use it to work out the name of the company she works for?

**GEMMA EVANS**
Relationship Manager

#  SPLIT DECISION

Back at the police station, Heather sees her colleague Danni Alvarez, and asks how she's getting on. They've only known each other for a month, but they're already as thick as thieves.

"Well, I've started manifesting, Hev."

"How very new age of you, Danni! How's that working out for you?"

"I've been telling myself daily for the last couple of weeks I deserve to be wealthy… and I'm still sitting here on a cop's salary with a massive rent bill to pay, so…"

"It's a work in progress then?" Heather offers as a cheery intervention.

She asks her colleague to check the records and confirm that Gemma and Dennis Baker got divorced six years ago. But there is no record of them being divorced on file. Was Gemma lying to her, and if so, what was her motivation for doing so?

Not for the first time on this case, something isn't adding up.

Look at the cards, which don't make the correct total. Can you swap a pair of cards to make the equation correct?

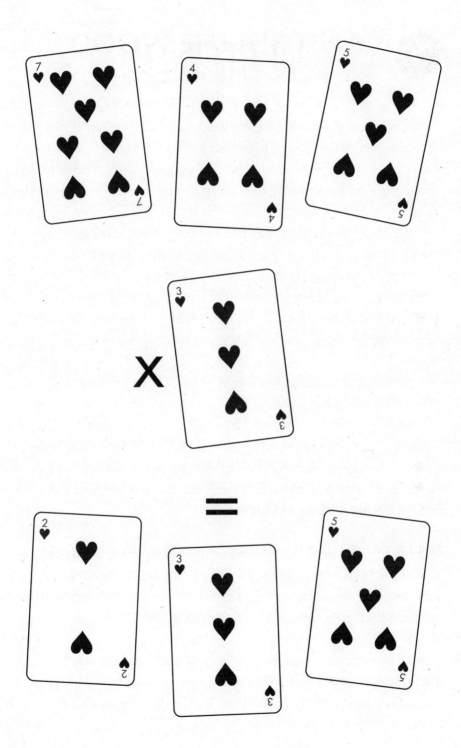

# 20 CAN'T SEE THE WOOD FOR THE TREES

Heather goes for a drive to clear her head and help her think through everything she's discovered so far. Along the way she stops at a local café to treat herself to a bacon sandwich for lunch, despite her hearty breakfast. A smug feeling comes over her as the owner asks if she'd like ketchup with it – at 50p a sachet. Heather politely declines then returns to her car with the sandwich, opens the glovebox, rummages past some handcuffs and pulls out a bottle of ketchup. As if she'd pay 50p for some ketchup! The previous time she'd been to the café she'd had no choice but to pay, and had almost nicked the owner for extortion. Now she's wise to the ketchup con, she always keeps a bottle with her.

She slathers the ketchup on top of the crispy bacon and is about take a bite when her phone rings.

"What is it with people calling me when I'm trying to eat?" she mutters, before taking that bite of the sandwich anyway and then desperately trying to chew and swallow it as quickly as she can before the phone goes to voicemail.

Fortunately she manages to answer the call in time, as after being told off for eating whilst on the phone, she is informed that a new piece of evidence has been found in some woodland near the millpond. Heather hotfoots it to the location.

The tree where the evidence has been found is surrounded (including diagonally) by six light-grey trees and two dark-grey trees. Can you identify the correct tree in the diagram?

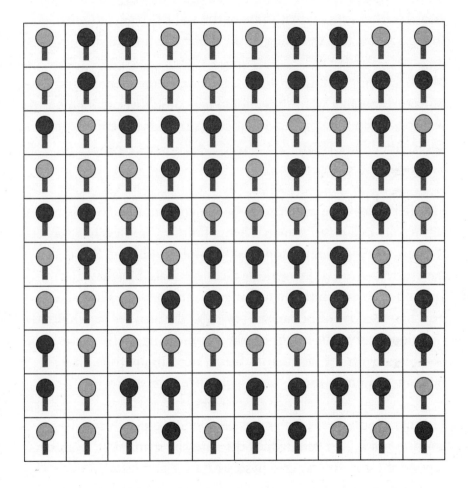

#  SCENTING BLOOD

On reaching the correct spot, Heather is informed that a few drops of blood have been found on a rock. Looking around the area, Heather can see that some of the soil has been loosened, as though a hole had been dug in the ground and filled in.

Heather hangs around for hours listening to the scene of crime officers discussing what they should and shouldn't catalogue, and watches a photographer taking pictures from every conceivable angle. The blood is sampled and sent off for testing to try to ascertain who it belongs to.

Heather knows she will need to be patient and wait to see if the test results in a positive match being found. Darkness has almost set in, so she decides to stop in at the pub for dinner. She does have a freezer full of low-calorie healthy meals, but they don't appeal to her any more than that gym membership she'd taken out then used twice before she gave up. She justifies her choice by the thought that she might overhear something useful at the pub, combined with the fact that it doesn't need to provide calorie information on its menus, and ignorance is bliss.

Heather's route to the pub takes her along a typically winding country road. Can you deduce the path the road takes? Numbers around the edge of the grid indicate how many sections of road are placed in each row/column of the grid. The road cannot cross itself, and if it visits a square, it either passes straight through it or turns at a right angle inside it.

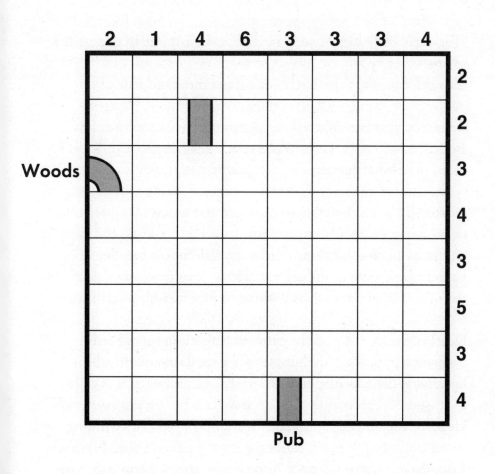

# PUB GRUB

As Heather walks to the bar she is greeted by the owner, Gus, with the words:

"You can't keep away, I see!" He seems slightly agitated, perhaps worried that he will be subjected to more questions, but Heather reassures him she is just here for a quiet meal and a drink.

Reassured that she is just there as a punter, Gus smiles at her and takes her order. Heather sits down at a free table and tries to listen in to what the regulars are talking about, but it all seems rather dull: something about Canada geese taking over the school sports field from the table to her right and a rant about waiting times at the doctors from the table to her left. Clearly the small matter of a definite murder and potential double murder in Upper Gorsetown is already yesterday's news for these residents as the minutiae of daily life is dominating their conversations.

Heather decides to pass the time waiting for her spaghetti bolognese by solving the puzzle in the local newspaper, the *Gorsetown Gazette*. She chuckles when she sees what it is called – killer sudoku! Hopefully she can solve this puzzle even if she can't yet solve the murder.

Place the numbers 1-9 once in each row, column and 3x3 bold-outlined box. The values of the squares in dotted-line regions must sum to the number given at the start of that region, and numbers cannot repeat inside them.

# GORSETOWN GAZETTE

| | | | | | | | | |
|---|---|---|---|---|---|---|---|---|
| 11 | 22 | | | 9 | | | 12 | |
| | 7 | | 19 | 13 | | 9 | | |
| | 8 | 13 | | | 9 | | 18 | 7 |
| 14 | | | 14 | | | 14 | | |
| | 11 | | 5 | 15 | | | | 9 |
| | 18 | | | 11 | 6 | | 13 | |
| 14 | | | 13 | | | | | 10 |
| 14 | 5 | 7 | | 10 | 15 | 12 | | |
| | | | | | | 18 | | |

# 23 CARELESS WHISPERS

Things are looking up for Heather. She's just solved the killer sudoku in short order and also read in the newspaper that one of her favourite TV shows has just been recommissioned. She decides to have another drink (non-alcoholic of course, as she will have to drive home later).

As she waits to be served at the bar, her ears prick up. A cleaner has just come out of the ladies' toilets with a note in hand and is showing it to the barman. She earwigs and apparently the cleaner just found it when emptying the rubbish bin, which they do every few days. Whether it got there by accident or was purposely disposed of is unclear.

Heather immediately strides over and explains who she is, and the cleaner gives her the note. It's in code, but Heather cracks it fairly easily. She then whisks the note straight over to the station for fingerprint testing overnight. Can you work out what the note says?

PHHW PH DW
WKH XVXDO
ORFDWLRQ. VLA
WKLUWB SP.
XUJHQW.

#  THE FINE PRINT

The next morning Heather wakes up thinking about the wording on the note. Who was arranging to meet someone else secretly, and why? Hoping her subconscious would work its magic and somehow provide her with the answer, she heads to the police station. As is often the case, she is greeted cheerily by her effervescent colleague, Danni. Her opening gambit is:

"There you are, Hev! I don't think we've ever had the biscuit debate, have we? Where do you stand on digestives? Underrated, aren't they? Granted they're nothing spectacular, but they get the job done."

Heather is normally more than happy to indulge such conversations – and come to think of it she does love a digestive – but as she is about to reply another colleague comes over and informs them that not only has a fingerprint been successfully extracted from the note, it has already been identified! Can you work out who matches the fingerprint?

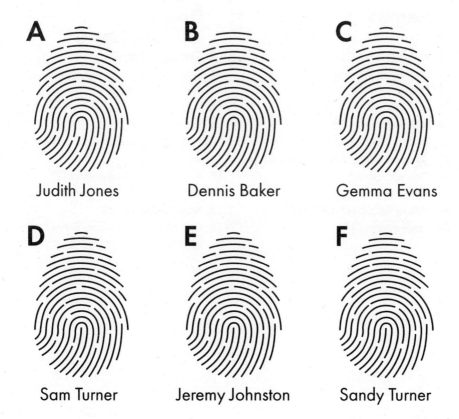

A — Judith Jones

B — Dennis Baker

C — Gemma Evans

D — Sam Turner

E — Jeremy Johnston

F — Sandy Turner

# (25) A MAN OF CONVICTION

Heather is intrigued – so the person who found Dennis Baker's body is also the person who left this clandestine note in the pub. Furthermore, she didn't take his fingerprints when talking to him which means that he must have a prior conviction! She really should have checked to see if there was a file on him before, an oversight that she quickly corrects.

Solve this crossword to reveal what his conviction was for.

## Across

**7** Observing (6)
**8** Victor (6)
**10** Located in the fresh air (7)
**11** Consecrate (5)
**12** Volcano in Sicily (4)
**13** Attendant upon God (5)
**17** Danger (5)
**18** Circle around the head of a saint (4)
**22** Steam room (5)
**23** Flatter (7)
**24** In slow tempo (of music) (6)
**25** Large lizard (6)

## Down

**1** Very loyal; dedicated (7)
**2** Taking a break (7)
**3** Gold block (5)
**4** Took small bites out of (7)
**5** Leg joints (5)
**6** Put clothes on (5)
**9** Foremost; main (9)
**14** Israeli city (3,4)
**15** Vehicle without an engine (7)
**16** Horse's fodder container (7)
**19** Academy award (5)
**20** One of the United Arab Emirates (5)
**21** What a mycologist studies (5)

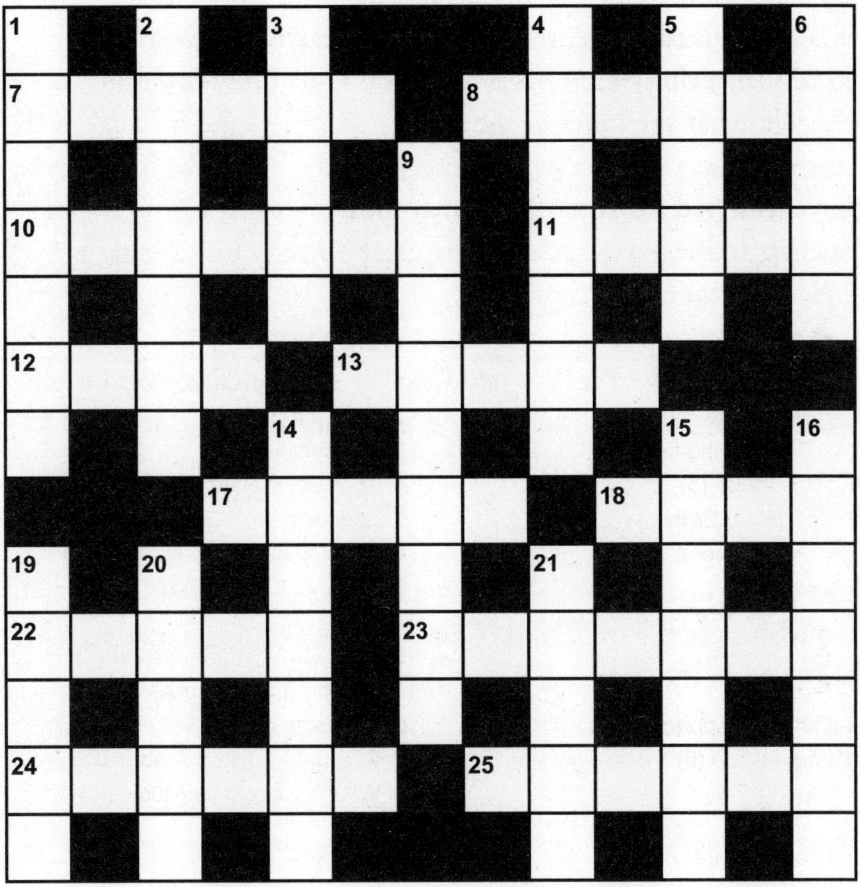
1
2
3
4
5
6
7
8
9
10
11
12
13
14
15
16
17
18
19
20
21
22
23
24
25

# DNA TEST

Heather goes and gets a coffee from the office machine whilst she thinks things through. It tastes like dishwater as usual, so she buys a chocolate bar to disguise the taste. She wonders why it is that vending machine coffee always tastes so awful: it seems to be something of a universal law. Taking a bite out of the chocolate bar she looks at the wrapper and sees the message 'to be consumed as part of a healthy diet', which she thinks is just code for 'this is bad for you – but you're going to eat it anyway!' She resents all those red circles that appear on tasty foods making you feel guilty for eating them.

As Heather chews on the chocolate bar she multitasks and mulls over what it might mean that the fingerprint belongs to Jeremy Johnston and whether the fact he has a previous conviction is relevant.

Just then, the results of the test on the blood found under the trees near the millpond comes in. The DNA has matched someone in the database. Solve the puzzle to find out whose blood it is:

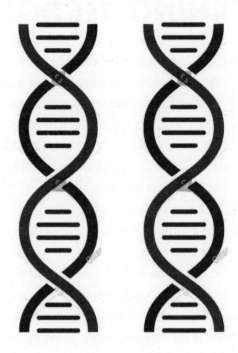

T-G-C

T-C-A-A

T-G-C-A-A

T-C-C

T-A

T

T-C-A-A

T-C-C

# 27 JOINING THE DOTS

The blood is Jeremy's! Heather was hoping it would be Dennis's blood so that it might provide some more clues as to what had happened to him before he met his maker, but alas not.

Taken together with the strange note bearing his fingerprint in the pub, it is now clear that Heather needs to speak to Mr. Johnston again, but this time not just for a chat. Why was his blood found near the site of the body? What was the strange note in the pub all about? Knowing that his childhood friends were planning to usurp him as head of the foraging society must have stung, but would it lead him to kill them? Heather has observed over the years that people have a penchant for getting the most irate about the most trivial of things: whether it be the font used for a new road sign or the colour of the bunting used at the summer fete, nothing gets people hot under the collar like the small details. Maybe the thought of losing his role at the foraging society to men he thought of as good friends was a big enough deal to kill over.

As Heather drives over to talk to Jeremy she gets stuck in traffic. It soon transpires there are roadworks en route. She had hoped moving to the countryside she'd avoid having to deal with those really annoying temporary traffic lights that always turn red just as you reach them and then stay red seemingly forever even though there's nothing coming the other way, but no such luck. At least the bumper sticker of the car in front of her – which reads 'Life's not hard, you're just soft' – makes her chuckle.

As she's waiting, she works out the questions she wants to ask Jeremy and mentally tries to connect the dots relating to the case so far.

Can you pair up all the black and white dots in this puzzle? Each white circle must be linked to exactly one black circle with a straight line running horizontally or vertically. Lines cannot cross each other. The puzzle can be solved logically.

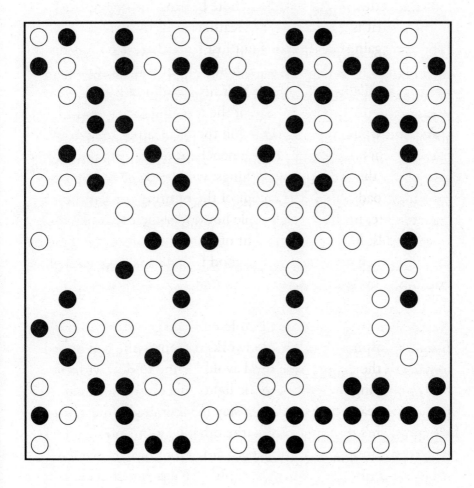

# 28 TAKE NOTE

As Heather arrives at Jeremy's home she finds him doing some gardening, whistling a cheery tune. Apparently he is not thinking about the deaths of his two friends at the moment.

"No brandy this time?" she enquires, to break the ice.

"Ha, no, not this morning!" he rejoinders. He looks mildly surprised to see her, and is remarkably chipper given the events of yesterday. He stands up and shakes her hand. Heather reciprocates automatically, only to then look down and notice all the dirt under his nails. She quickly takes out some hand sanitiser and tries to squirt it on her hands without him noticing and taking offence. She fails miserably and Jeremy chuckles and apologises, saying: "Ah, sorry about that! I see that bottle says it kills 99% of bacteria. Let's hope the other 1% are harmless ones!"

Heather chuckles – "I've wondered the same thing myself. Killing 99% probably means there are still millions left, doesn't it! I bet the 1% are the really bad ones!"

Jeremy nods, then says, "And how can I help you today? I'm assuming this is not a social visit."

Heather informs him that some drops of his blood have been found near the location where he found the body of Dennis Baker. Jeremy nonchalantly tells her this is no surprise, as he regularly goes walking through the forest, either just for exercise or looking for mushrooms, and he occasionally catches himself on something sharp like a branch, perhaps when bending down to examine something on the floor. He vaguely recalls something like that happening recently when his foot collapsed in some loose soil and needing to put a plaster on a small cut when he got home.

This sounds plausible enough to Heather – for now, at least. She imagines that if he had been fighting Dennis Baker there would be more blood than a couple of drops, and presumably some of Baker's too. She then asks if he is aware his friends were plotting to overthrow him as chairman of the foraging society. He admits to being slightly annoyed by it, but it's hardly something to kill over. With Jeremy thus far remaining calm and poised, she moves on to the mysterious note – who did he want to meet at the 'usual location', and why was it urgent?

Jeremy suddenly looks flustered and his face turns red.

"How on earth did you find that note?" he sputters. Heather explains it was found in the pub. Jeremy nods as though that makes sense, although he says nothing directly about it.

Heather presses him as to who the note was for. He looks around the garden and the surrounding area, checking there is no-one within earshot, then whispers the name to her using a code he is sure she will understand.

Solve this puzzle to reveal who he was seeing.

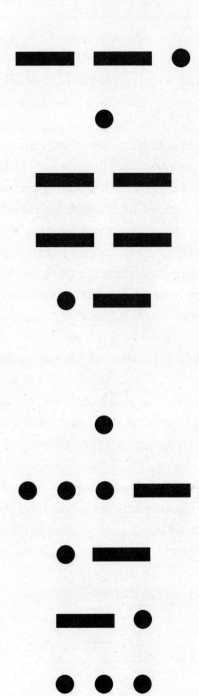

# 29 MEETING IN SECRET

Jeremy Johnston explains that he is in a relationship with Gemma Evans! "But why the secrecy?" Heather enquires.

"Well, that was a cause of some frustration to me. Gemma always wanted to keep it quiet – she didn't want Dennis to find out that she had moved on, you see. Naturally I found that frustrating and slightly suspicious. I kept asking her why and she said it was because she was technically still married and she thought Dennis might take it badly if he found out she was seeing a friend of his. She said he might get jealous or annoyed with one or both of us and it wasn't worth the hassle. I'm not sure why, but for whatever reason they had never actually divorced."

Heather asks Jeremy when he had written the note asking Gemma to meet him at 'the usual location'.

He replies as follows:

"Now that is rather more straightforward. If it were now the day after tomorrow, then I would have left the note the day before the day before the day before the day that was two days before."

Heather thinks about it for a while, and notes down how many days ago he had written the note. When was it?

# (30) UNDER DISCUSSION

Heather has worked out from Mr. Johnston's cryptic answer that he had arranged to meet up with Gemma the night before he had found Dennis Baker's body. The timing does seem more than a little suspicious.

Jeremy explains that Gemma often goes to the pub for a lunchtime drink so he went to surreptitiously give her the note there to ask her to meet up with him that evening. He was in the pub for a matter of minutes, if that. He knew if he spoke to her openly, she might get annoyed given the clandestine nature of their relationship. Evidently she must have read it, put it in her pocket and it fell out when she went to use the facilities.

Heather asks what it was in particular that he wanted to discuss with such urgency.

Solve this kriss kross to find out. Place each of the words once into the grid, then take the letters in shaded squares to spell out what Jeremy wanted to talk about.

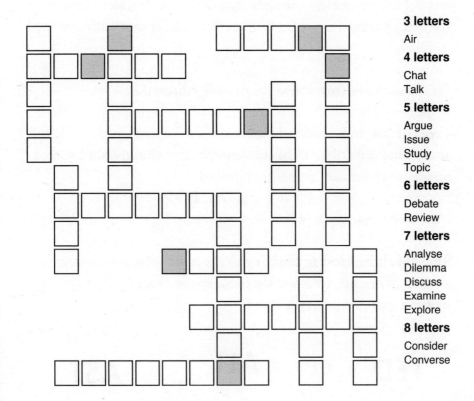

**3 letters**
Air

**4 letters**
Chat
Talk

**5 letters**
Argue
Issue
Study
Topic

**6 letters**
Debate
Review

**7 letters**
Analyse
Dilemma
Discuss
Examine
Explore

**8 letters**
Consider
Converse

# 31 DIVORCED FROM REALITY

Jeremy explains that a friend of his had seen Gemma talking to Dennis in whispers, as though the two of them were sharing a secret. He had just about been prepared to keep their relationship a secret from Dennis, at Gemma's request, but this was the last straw. He demanded to see her and find out once and for all if she was committed to him or if she was still emotionally attached to Dennis.

Heather asks Jeremy where they arranged to meet.

"Well, it had to be somewhere away from prying eyes, of course, as Gemma didn't like to be seen in public with me – she's such a puzzle, that woman, an enigma indeed."

"Anyhow, I ask again, where did you meet?"

Three of the following word segments can be combined to create a word. Work out which three those are in order to discover where he arranged to meet Gemma.

TED       ALL        AST

ISM

CAT

ENT

SIM       FUL

OTM       PET

# 32 A STING IN THE TAIL

Jeremy says, "I got there early, at around sixish, but Gemma was already there, pacing up and down by the beehives. I got the impression she'd been there a while, possibly thinking through what to say."

Heather asks what happened next.

"I'm a truthful person, detective, you know?"

Heather doesn't reply to this question, which is probably rhetorical – and she finds silence can be powerful sometimes. She wants to get as much information as she can from Jeremy, but she has found from experience that people who like to let it be known they are truthful often are the readiest to tell a lie or two.

After a pregnant pause, Jeremy continues:

"We had a heart to heart that must have lasted hours. I thought things were getting resolved, but then before I knew it we were having a rather heated argument. I asked her what she had been talking to Dennis in whispers about. I reminded her that when we got together there was no love lost between her and Dennis, and she seemed quite open to the idea of him finding out about us, and even going public with our relationship. Well, I've noticed lately she's been rather nice to him when she's seen him – I had to challenge her about it, didn't I?"

Heather is about to ask a question when Jeremy carries on:

"She was very defensive, kept telling me to mind my own business, and why was I snooping on her and that sort of thing. Then she hesitated and I thought she was going to say something, maybe divulge something to explain her behaviour, like some secret, you know?"

"We all have our secrets, Mr. Johnston," Heather opines wisely.

"That's as may be. Anyhow, she seemed to change her mind and just got annoyed with me again. We got nowhere and in the end she stormed off, saying she wasn't sure about us anymore. I'm not too sure where we stand now, to be honest."

"And where did you both go after that?"

"I went home – I'm assuming Gemma did the same. I wouldn't want to have met her in a dark alley the mood she was in, that's for sure!"

Heather asks what time the argument finished. Solve the puzzle to determine the time. Squares containing numbers indicate how many of the adjacent squares (including diagonally-adjacent squares) and the square itself must be shaded. Therefore a zero means that neither the square itself nor any of its neighbours are shaded, whilst a 9 in a square would mean that the square itself and all eight neighbours are shaded.

| | | 3 | 4 | 3 | | 1 | | | 3 | | | | |
|---|---|---|---|---|---|---|---|---|---|---|---|---|---|
| | 5 | | | 4 | | 1 | | 3 | 6 | | | 5 | 4 |
| 4 | | 3 | | | | 1 | | 3 | | | 3 | | |
| | 4 | 3 | | | | 4 | | 6 | | | 3 | | 3 |
| | 6 | | | 5 | 4 | 1 | | | 6 | | 5 | | |
| | 3 | 3 | | | | 1 | | | | 3 | | 3 | 2 |
| | | | 3 | 2 | | | 1 | | | | | 3 | 1 |
| | 2 | 3 | 3 | | | 2 | 1 | | | | | 1 | |
| | | | | | 4 | | 3 | | 0 | 1 | 3 | | |
| 3 | 4 | | | 5 | | | | | | 2 | | | |
| 3 | | 5 | 3 | | | 6 | 4 | | | | | 4 | |
| 3 | 4 | | | | 3 | | | 2 | | | 4 | | |
| | | | | | | | 3 | | | 1 | 3 | | |
| 3 | | 3 | | 0 | | 3 | | | | 0 | | | 3 |
| | | | 0 | | 0 | | 2 | | | | 2 | | |

# (33) ENTRY REQUIREMENTS

Heather needs to establish an alibi for Jeremy for the rest of the evening and overnight, but he receives an urgent call – apparently his mother has been taken ill. Heather lets him head off but makes it clear she still has more to ask him.

Heather takes stock of what she knows. Jeremy has been seeing Dennis Baker's ex-wife, Gemma, and is clearly annoyed that she seems to be on friendly terms with Dennis again and won't commit to their relationship. Did he decide to kill Dennis Baker to get him out of the picture? And why was Gemma being friendly to her ex and wearing the wedding ring again? Interestingly, Jeremy didn't mention the latter – perhaps he hadn't noticed. And how did Sam Turner fit into the equation? Was his death related to that of Dennis or not, and had he accidentally poisoned himself or was the truth altogether more sinister? A cause of death for Sam seemed to be taking a long time to come through.

With all the questions spinning around her head, Heather decides to visit Gemma at her workplace and get her side of the story: it's important to see if her timings and version of events corroborate what Jeremy has told her. She heads there as quickly as she can, keen to get there before Jeremy can tip her off that she might well be paid a visit. Depending on how truthful he's been with her, Heather considers this a real possibility: the two of them could be in cahoots, somehow.

When she arrives at the premises of AlgoFill, the tech company where Gemma works, there is a prominent sign by the entrance gate that reads "This gate is manned at all times – buzz if you need any help." Despite the sign, there is nobody at the gate to wave her through as a police officer. She must instead work out the entry code herself. Can you work out the four-digit code using the information from five incorrect guesses to help you make progress? Each digit in the code is different. A tick indicates that a number appears in the code and in the correct place, whilst a question mark indicates that a number appears in the code but in a different place. You must work out which number is being referred to by each of the ticks and question marks on each line.

3602: ??

9408: ✓✓ ?

1579: ?

2403: ✓ ??

3916: ?

#  HOT DESKING

The gate swings open, and Heather enquires at reception as to where she might find Gemma. She is told that the AlgoFill office layout is rather complicated.

"But fear not," says the receptionist optimistically, if not convincingly, "the floorplan was created by a state-of-the-art algorithm so there is exactly one way and one way only to reach any desk and to move between any pair of desks in the office. We sit employees in a different location each week to keep things interesting: we find it benefits the quality of their work. One snag: the algorithm was supposed to only require you to use the stairs once but it glitched slightly, so you might find yourself having to walk up and down staircases several times." Heather grimaces, and the receptionist adds, slightly unconvincingly, "On the positive side, it's good for your fitness!"

She proceeds to print Heather a map of the two floors of the office and marks the location of Gemma's desk with a picture of a human. Plot the route Heather must take from the reception on the ground floor (left-hand diagram) to Gemma's desk on the first floor (right-hand diagram). Where you see a staircase symbol (>) on the lower floor, you may choose to walk up to the same location on the first floor, or pass straight through the square and not use the stairs. Likewise, where you see a staircase symbol (<) on the upper floor, you can choose to walk down the stairs if you wish.

**Reception**

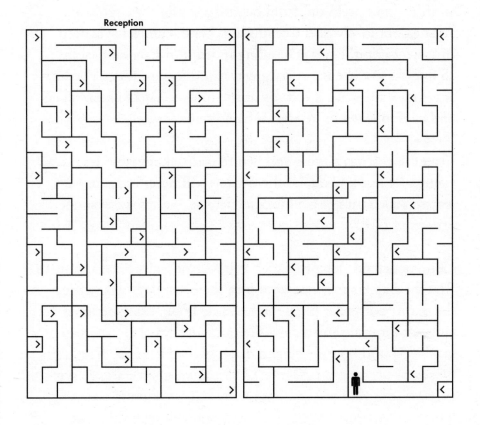

# 35 HUSH, HUSH

As she (finally) nears Gemma's desk, cursing the algorithm under her breath and worrying about the day our AI masters take over the world, Heather hears hushed voices squabbling. She moves stealthily and peeks out from behind a stationery cupboard. As she does so, she sees Gemma and her daughter Layla deep in conversation. Layla is standing in front of a verdant cactus so it looks like she has spiky green hair. Heather stifles a laugh, realising she'd make a bad spy as she finds it hard to keep quiet, and tries to listen in to what is being said.

"You know I was hoping you would get back together with Dad eventually," says Layla, "and now that will never happen. I bet Jeremy killed him to get him out the way, he always seemed jealous of Dad!"

Gemma defends Jeremy, which is interesting given the argument that she'd apparently had with him the other day. Heather jots down one particular phrase in her note book, using her own singular form of shorthand. What does it say?

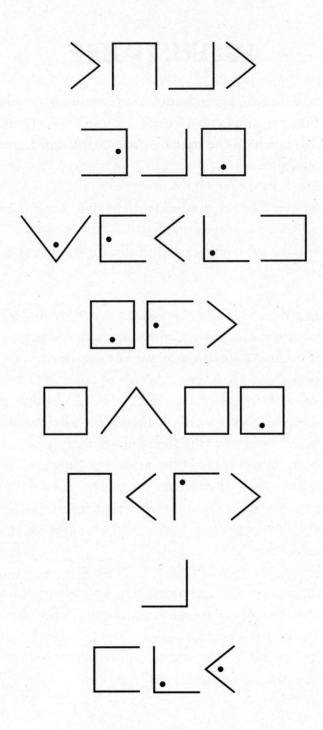

# WORKER BEE

Heather continues to loiter, but the conversation dies down and then she hears Gemma start tapping away at her keyboard. She steps out from behind the stationery cupboard, and Gemma does a double-take.

"How long have you been standing there, detective?" she asks.

"Long enough," says Heather cryptically. Layla looks at her with suspicion.

Heather asks directly if Gemma saw Jeremy the night before Dennis Baker was murdered. Gemma nods, and confirms they did indeed arrange to meet up by the beehives at the local allotments at around 6:30pm, although in point of fact they both arrived early. She explains she hates being late due to her childhood experiences. Her mum always got her to school just as the gates were closing and she found all the rushing around very stressful. She also didn't like being known by the other students as 'the late kid'. She had asked her mum if they could simply leave home a few minutes earlier each day and her mum looked astonished at the suggestion – she was late for everything and had no problem with it.

"Anyway, I wasn't in the best mood, and I got stung by a bee for my troubles. We had an argument about our relationship and, of course, Dennis. I don't think Dennis would be very happy that we are together and Layla isn't too fond of Jeremy because he's not her Dad. So... it's complicated!"

"Most relationships are," proffers Heather, before adding, "And what time did you leave?" She is keen to see if Gemma's story tallies with Jeremy's.

Solve this puzzle to find her answer.

Each hexagonal cell of the beehive contains a different letter. Some letters have already been placed to get you started. You must place each letter shown underneath the beehive once each. When the letters are in place it should be possible to make each word shown alongside the grid by moving from hexagon to adjacent hexagon. The answer will be revealed in the numbered squares.

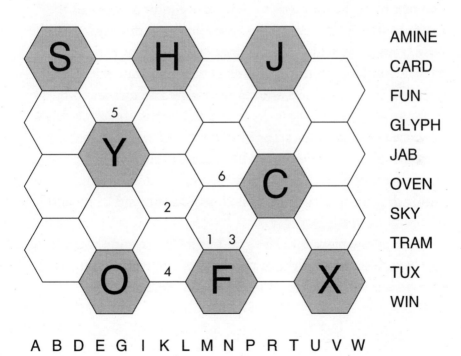

AMINE
CARD
FUN
GLYPH
JAB
OVEN
SKY
TRAM
TUX
WIN

A B D E G I K L M N P R T U V W

# MOVIE NIGHT

Heather notes this down. The time pretty much tallies with that given by Jeremy – is ten minutes significant? It's hard to see how, really. She now needs to find out if Gemma has an alibi for the rest of the night, and therefore if she can be ruled out as a prime suspect.

"Where did you go after the argument?" Heather asks.

"I went straight home and then watched a couple of movies with Layla before going to bed."

"Which films did you watch?" Heather enquires. She had discovered over the years that someone telling the truth would answer instantly whilst a liar would take longer as they had to make up facts on the spot, unless they had anticipated the question in advance and already formulated an answer.

"*Pride and Prejudice* and *The Ugly Truth*," replies Gemma, frustratingly not answering quickly but not slowly either.

"And what time did you go to bed, would you say?"

Fit each jigsaw piece into the grid to spell a common word in each of the six rows of the grid. You may not rotate the pieces. The answer will be revealed in the shaded squares.

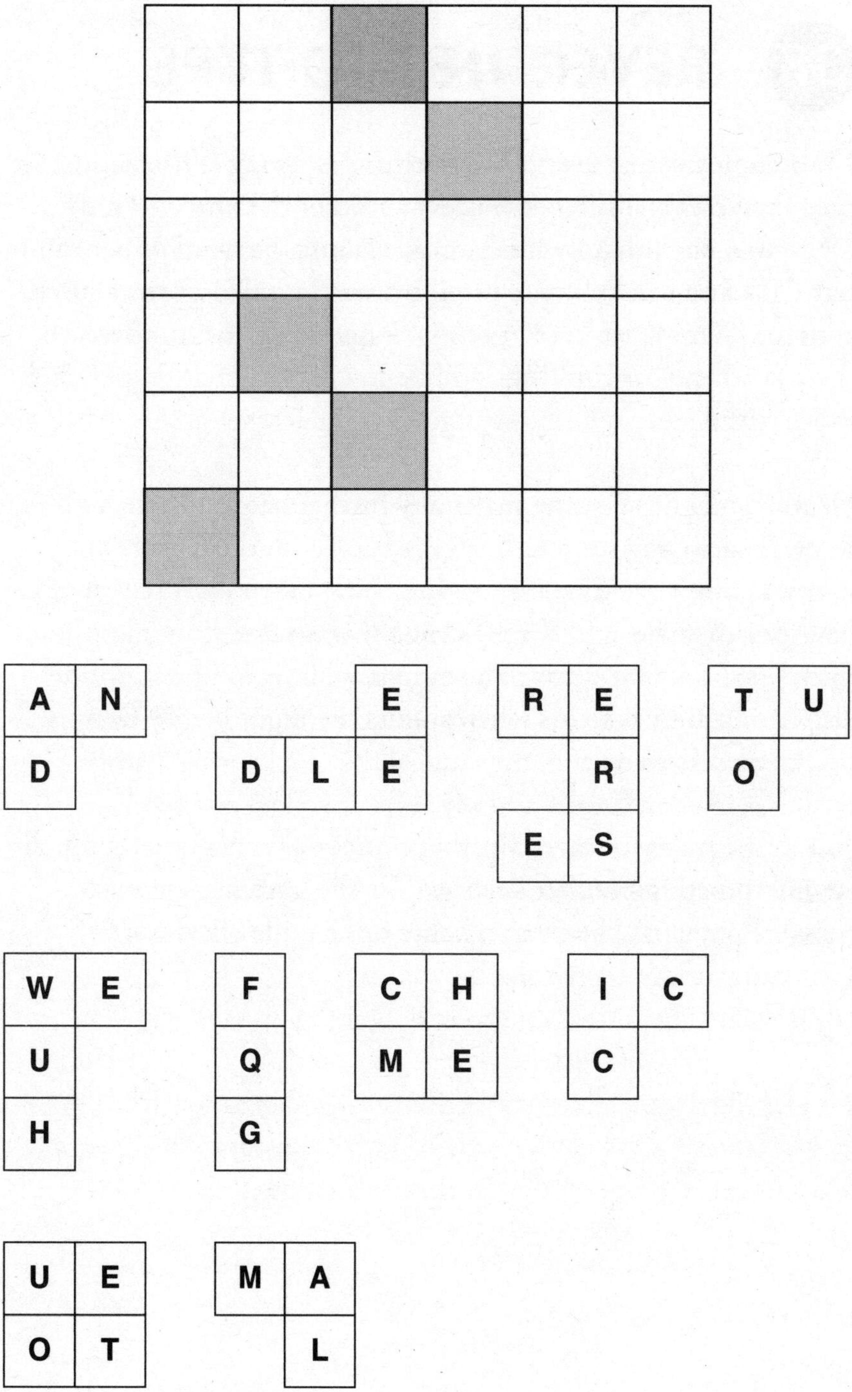
A N
D
E
D L E
R E
R
E S
T U
O
W E
U
H
F
Q
G
C H
M E
I C
C
U E
O T
M A
L

# 38 REVERTING TO TYPE

Layla confirms that everything Gemma is saying is true, and they then had a leisurely breakfast together the next morning. Of course, she is hardly likely to go against the word of her mum, but – if Layla can be trusted – this does seem like a pretty surefire alibi for Gemma, at least in terms of her being the murderer. Is she a dead end, or could she still be involved somehow, perhaps indirectly?

Heather decides she can't make any further progress here, and resolves to go and see Jeremy again and finish the conversation that was interrupted by his mother being taken ill. A few hours have passed since, and she is hoping it was something minor and Jeremy is back home now. She urgently needs to find out if he also has an alibi as to his whereabouts the night before Dennis' body was discovered.

Just as she turns to leave, Heather notices Gemma quietly touch-typing something on her keyboard. Is she sending Jeremy a message perhaps? She catches some of Gemma's keypresses. Can you work out what she typed?

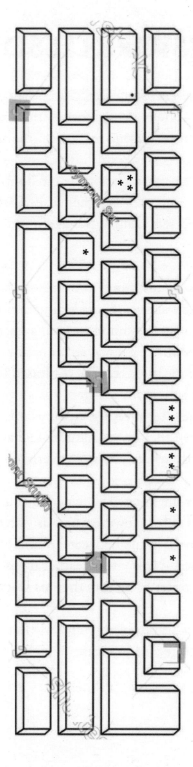

#  HISTORY LESSON

As she pulls up at Jeremy's house, she sees the curtains twitch. Heather is pleased as he is clearly back home. He doesn't open the door to her, instead waiting for her to ring the bell.

"What a surprise!" he says as he opens the door, emphasising that it's a surprise so strongly that Heather suspects it is anything but. Perhaps Gemma did send him a message warning him that she was on her way...

Heather enquires as to his mum, and he says that fortunately it was nothing to worry about: she had fainted quite dramatically, but it turned out to be a response to some new medication she was taking, which would easily be remedied by trying her on a different medicine. Heather says she is pleased to hear it, and then gets straight to the point: "I need to ask you what you did when you got home after meeting Gemma at the allotments, Jeremy. Clearly given the serious nature of what has happened, I need to know exactly where you were overnight."

Jeremy says that, as she knows, he lives alone, and so nobody can corroborate his alibi. However, he was watching videos on the internet for several hours between around 9:30pm until 2am when he went to bed. He invites Heather to check the browser history on his computer to be sure that his story checks out.

Heather looks at his search history and works out how to extract one letter from each record to create an eight-letter word. Is he telling the truth?

21:30 QUANTUM PHYSICS FOR STARTERS [42 MINUTES]

 22:12 GREAT CAT VIDEOS [12 MINUTES]

 22:24 COMMERCE AND BUSINESS NEWS [32 MINUTES]

 22:56 GARDENING TIPS AND TRICKS [41 MINUTES]

 23:37 FORAGING FOR MUSHROOMS [34 MINUTES]

 00:11 MAKE YOUR RELATIONSHIPS FANTASTIC [41 MINUTES]

 00:52 RUGBY UNION ROUNDUP [36 MINUTES]

 01:28 ADVICE ON SLEEPING WELL [32 MINUTES]

#  THE TRUTH WILL OUT

The following morning Heather heads straight to the police station. It looks to her as though Gemma has a credible alibi as to where she was all night and Jeremy has one until at least 2am. Depending on the time the murder was committed, which she is still waiting on, this could go a long way to ruling them both out of her enquiries into Dennis's murder. As for Sam – she now really needs to know if it was a case of accidental poisoning or something more sinister. Once she knows that, she will know definitively if the two events are linked, which will really help her continue the investigation.

As she walks through the door of the station, she is greeted cheerily by her colleague Danni. Heather sees she's reading a detective novel which she justifies as being 'work-related', if not exactly what she's paid for. Heather reads a line aloud: "If you want to understand the future of a case then first you must look to the past. Everything that will happen is borne out of seeds planted then, if only you have the nous to find them."

Danni nods silently, before adding: "Good, isn't it. I've no idea what it means, or how it helps you solve a case, but that's not the point of a novel, I suppose." She then adds, almost as an afterthought:

"What do you make of the will reading, Hev?"

"What will reading?" Heather replies – no-one tells her anything around here!

"Ah – you didn't know. Bit awkward. Well it's come out that Dennis Baker left his entire estate to just one person. Can you guess who?"

Solve this puzzle to find out who is set to inherit Dennis Baker's estate. To do so, you must shade some squares in the grid. Numbers in squares specify how many neighbouring squares should be shaded in – including diagonally touching squares. Squares that contain numbers must not be shaded.

|   |   |   |   |   |   |   |   |   |   |
|---|---|---|---|---|---|---|---|---|---|
|   |   | 0 |   |   | 4 |   | 4 |   |   |
|   | 3 |   |   | 8 |   |   | 7 |   | 3 |
|   |   | 0 |   |   |   |   |   |   |   |
|   | 5 |   |   | 7 | 4 | 4 |   |   | 1 |
|   |   |   |   |   |   |   |   |   |   |
|   |   |   | 3 | 1 |   |   | 4 |   |   |
| 0 |   |   | 2 | 0 |   |   |   |   | 2 |
|   |   |   | 3 |   | 3 |   |   | 5 | 3 |
| 0 |   |   |   |   |   |   |   | 5 | 3 |
|   | 3 |   | 3 | 0 |   |   |   |   |   |
| 0 |   |   | 5 |   | 1 | 3 | 5 | 5 | 3 |
|   |   |   |   |   |   |   |   | 2 |   |

# 41 PROFIT MOTIVE

Heather notes that this news counts in Gemma's favour – she didn't stand to directly benefit from Dennis's will. That removes the profit motive, unless of course she didn't know she'd been cut out of the will at some point since their not-quite-divorce. Heather reasons that it is out of the question that Layla would kill her own Dad and she would have been unlikely to have known the contents of his will anyway; 18-year-olds surely don't think about that sort of thing.

Heather keeps an open mind about Gemma, notwithstanding her alibi corroborated by her daughter. If she somehow knew about the will change, perhaps she had started being nice to Dennis to persuade him to change his mind, or possibly had him killed as revenge for being removed from the will. Motives can be murky and complicated.

Just then, Heather's inbox pings. It's the report from the coroner into Dennis Baker's cause of death. "I hope this provides some answers. What do you think it will say?" she asks Danni.

"Stabbing, obviously," says Danni, looking over her shoulder, before adding, "These coroners in cases like this – money for old rope, honestly!"

Some of the contents of the report are encoded, which makes sense given the sensitive information it contains. Can you crack the code to reveal this part of the message?

HT_EACSU_EFOD_AEHTO__
FEDNNSIB_KAREH_SAB_
EE_NSEATLBSIEH_DSAC_
NOUSPMITNOO__FOPSINOUO_
SUMHSORMO_SOCBMNIDEW_
TI_H_AAFAT_LNIUJYRR_
SELUITGNF_OR_MEBNI_
GTSBAEBD

# 42 MIND-BLOWING NEWS

Danni is forced to eat her words. Neither of them had foreseen this twist!

"So… both Sam and Dennis were poisoned by mushrooms, then?" she says, articulating exactly what Heather is thinking. She also notes that the coroner's report estimates Dennis's time of death as 6:30am.

Heather thinks out loud: "So why the stab wound as well, then? Is that misdirection? Or did something go wrong and that was to fix a botched job?"

Danni says: "Well, the two cases are clearly linked now, and chances are the same person killed them both. I don't think the idea that Sam accidentally cooked himself the wrong mushrooms is credible anymore – he was poisoned deliberately. And – in my opinion – you should be looking squarely at the members of the foraging society – clearly they'd have the expertise to poison someone and would also want to cover their tracks. I reckon the stabbing was a bluff to take your attention away from the fact it was poisoning, and to stop you looking too closely into members of that society. Who likes mushrooms that much anyway?"

Heather says nothing, but nods slowly. Is she missing something?

Find the missing letter in each of the six letter wheels to work out what, or who, Heather is thinking about. Each word reads clockwise around the wheel once the missing letter is added.

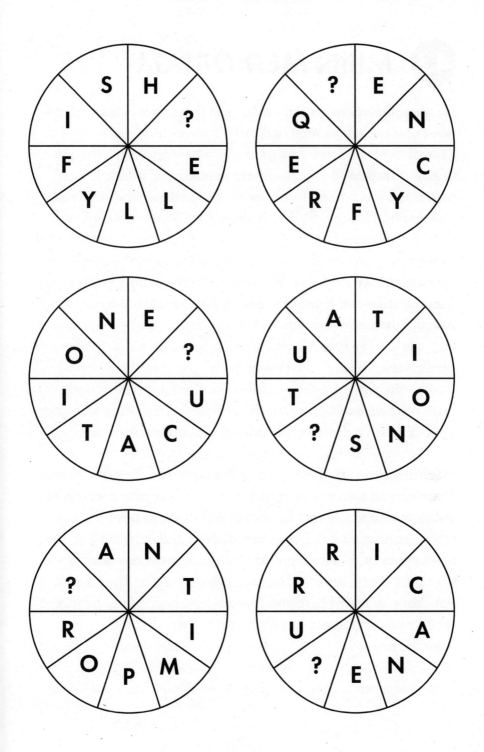

# IN MEMORIAM

Heather resolves to go and talk to Judith again in light of the news that both dead men had eaten poisonous mushrooms – as a member of the foraging society she would have the expertise to pull this off, and potentially the motive too. Whilst it was clear there was no love lost between her and Sam, perhaps she also resented Dennis for going along with Sam's scheme to get them elected to high office in the foraging society. However, that conversation will need to wait a little while, as in the afternoon the community are holding a memorial service for Dennis and Sam. Heather and Danni have been asked to attend by their boss, but told to keep a respectful distance so they don't come across as overly nosy. The funerals cannot be held yet as the bodies haven't been released back to the families.

Both men were religious, and Father Stibley, the priest from the local church, St. Brigid's, introduces the memorial service.

"Welcome, friends. The events of the last few days will have been disturbing and unsettling for all of us here in Upper Gorsetown. Today we come together to celebrate the lives of our brothers in Christ, Dennis Baker and Sam Turner. Today we are a community of disparate people united as one in our grief. They say that the days are long, but the years are short. The years of our dearly departed Sam and Dennis have ended in this life, but we take comfort in the fact their years in the next life are just beginning.

"The Bible tells us that there is a time for everything. There is a time to be born and a time to die. It also tells us that there is a time to weep and a time to laugh, a time to mourn and a time to dance. Friends, today I suggest we really do focus on celebrating the lives of Dennis and Sam; that we think more about dancing than mourning. Yes, tears and sadness are important parts of the grieving process, but just for this afternoon let's think about all that they have contributed to our lives…"

The priest's words start to drift out of Heather's consciousness as she is busy scanning the service to see who is there. As far as she can tell, everyone she expected to be there has turned up to the event: Layla, Jeremy, Judith, Sam's wife Sandy and other members of Sam's and Dennis' families, together with various local residents. She also spots Carol and most of the other members of the local foraging society. But where's Gemma? Ah, there she is – she's smiling broadly as she is being given a hug by the pub landlord, Gus, who must know everyone around these parts. She's wearing a very flowery and cheerful jumper given the solemnity of the occasion. Heather wonders if she is trying to signal that she isn't upset. Heather also observes there is no wedding ring on her finger.

Jeremy gets up and gives a short speech to those present. Solve the puzzle below to reveal the theme of his speech. Answer each crossword-style clue in the relevant row and the theme will be revealed in the shaded squares.

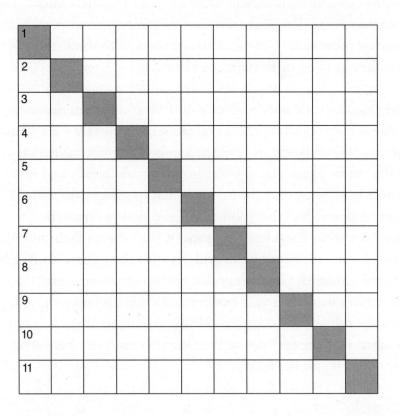

1. Person who tackles blazes

2. Difficult to understand or do

3. Tool; type of cocktail

4. Overstated

5. Thoughtful and concerned for others

6. Accomplishment

7. Person who might give you a trim

8. Unlucky

9. Instantly

10. Leading character in a novel

11. School subject with fractions

#  SAY IT WITH FLOWERS

It struck Heather as a little odd for Jeremy to be talking about forgiveness in his speech rather than focusing on paying tribute to his two dead friends. Was there a reason for this – guilt perhaps?

Outside the church, she is taken aback by the large number of bouquets of flowers and notes of tribute from local residents. Clearly these two men were well-liked and respected members of the community. The messages all seem to be exactly what you'd expect – short statements like 'in loving memory', 'taken too soon' and so forth.

One of the notes makes her chuckle. Find the correct route through the grid by identifying and following the chain of flower bouquets through the grid, moving one square at a time horizontally or vertically from the entry arrow to the exit arrow. Doing so will reveal who wrote the amusing message.

| F | L | O | W | E | R | E | B | O | E | E | O | W | L | O | U | Q | U | E | T |
|---|---|---|---|---|---|---|---|---|---|---|---|---|---|---|---|---|---|---|---|
| E | U | Q | U | O | B | F | R | U | B | E | L | E | Q | B | E | F | R | O | B |
| T | U | W | Q | T | F | O | E | Q | U | B | F | R | F | R | Q | L | O | E | O |
| F | T | B | W | Q | R | F | W | U | U | O | T | B | E | E | L | U | B | R | W |
| L | L | E | W | O | L | L | O | E | E | Q | E | O | L | W | O | L | F | T | E |
| O | R | W | L | L | O | F | L | T | T | O | U | U | O | F | F | F | W | B | U |
| W | R | O | W | E | R | O | F | F | Q | E | Q | Q | W | U | O | T | E | E | Q |
| E | E | L | F | T | B | U | T | L | U | O | U | U | B | W | L | B | W | O | U |
| R | U | U | Q | E | O | Q | E | O | O | Q | O | E | U | O | U | E | U | L | O |
| B | O | U | Q | U | U | Q | U | W | E | R | B | T | F | L | O | W | E | R | B |

# 45 SECRET CONFESSION

Gus Hawkins had written a little card that said: "Get the beers lined up for me in Heaven, gentlemen, I reckon I'll be joining you before last orders!" This is what made Heather chuckle.

"Glad you like it!" says Gus, as he sidles up alongside her. "So sad – the least I could do is try to bring a smile to the faces of those who read my little note." He then points out Gemma's jumper to Heather, saying it seems a little loud for an occasion such as this. Heather nods: she isn't the only person who has noticed, then.

Just then it starts raining gently. She thinks Gus is about to say something else, but then she hears another voice say: "Tears from heaven, someone once poetically told me." She turns around, having been looking up at the firmament, and she sees that Father Stibley has wandered over.

"Beautiful service, Father!" she says, although in truth she had been deep in thought for much of it. Danni walks over and joins them, whilst Gus heads off to talk to the families.

"The community are rather shaken by what has happened, as you can imagine," the priest replies. "I think it's really made people look at themselves and how they act. I've had several people come to me for confession these last couple of days, including one surprising name."

"And who was that, Father?" enquires Danni.

"Oh, perhaps I've said too much," says Father Stibley, looking a little flustered. "As you know, I'm bound by absolute confidentiality. I cannot say any more."

This is frustrating, but the priest is adamant his lips are sealed.

Heather's phone pings, and she receives a very important update. The mushrooms that Sam consumed before his untimely death have been identified. Furthermore, tests on Dennis have shown that he also ingested exactly the same type of mushroom. Solve this puzzle to reveal its name. All answers share the same set of seven letters. Answer the crossword-style clues to deduce the letters.

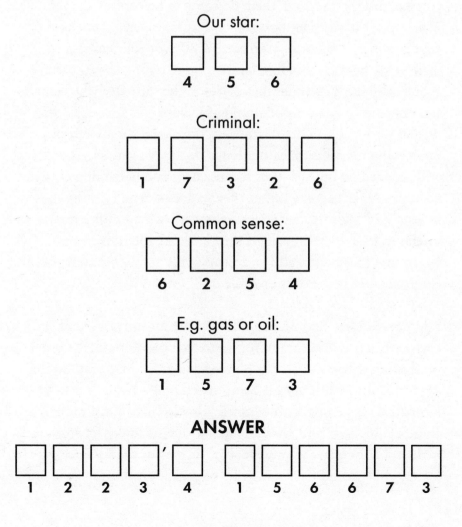

Our star:

| | | |
|---|---|---|
| 4 | 5 | 6 |

Criminal:

| | | | | |
|---|---|---|---|---|
| 1 | 7 | 3 | 2 | 6 |

Common sense:

| | | | |
|---|---|---|---|
| 6 | 2 | 5 | 4 |

E.g. gas or oil:

| | | | |
|---|---|---|---|
| 1 | 5 | 7 | 3 |

**ANSWER**

| | | | ' | | | | | | | |
|---|---|---|---|---|---|---|---|---|---|---|
| 1 | 2 | 2 | 3 | 4 | 1 | 5 | 6 | 6 | 7 | 3 |

# 46 NOBODY'S FOOL

Back at the police station, Heather's boss asks her for an update on the case. The timing is good, as Heather can mention this recent development that conclusively links together the two deaths. Her boss has a great poker face, and it is hard to tell if he is impressed by this news or not. He offers some sobering advice: "I once read that 90% of police detectives think they are in the top 10% at solving cases, Heather. Where do you think you are?" Heather ponders this for a second, then, deciding to be confident, says: "The top 10%, sir." Her boss responds impassively: "Let's hope your confidence is not as misplaced as 80% of your colleagues, then." Heather isn't sure that figure is quite right – there could be people who don't consider themselves in the top 10% who actually are, but decides against questioning her boss.

On leaving his office, Heather looks into fool's funnel. The fact it was ingested by both victims means she is surely looking at two possible scenarios now. Either they were accidental deaths caused by Sam and Dennis sharing a meal together, or a murderer somehow deliberately ensured they both ate the mushrooms. Given one of the men also ended up being stabbed, surely the latter scenario is the only credible one.

Heather decides she'd best read up on the mushrooms, and finds out that it is common for them to grow alongside another mushroom called the Scotch bonnet which is safe to eat. So she can't completely discount it being accidental – but it is much more likely someone with detailed knowledge of mushrooms chose deliberately and wisely. Sam and Dennis were far from fools when it comes to mushrooms. As part of the foraging society they would have had years of practice discriminating one type of mushroom from another, and she remembers Jeremy saying he was in awe of their knowledge in this field.

As she is pondering things, one of her colleagues comes over to her, breathless.

"You'll never guess what – while you and Danni were at the memorial service, we received an anonymous tip off to check the rubbish bins of that Judith Jones – you've spoken to her, haven't you? Anyhow, we've rummaged through her bins, and found some mushrooms in there that look to my amateur eye like fool's funnel! Of course I'll send them straight for testing, but this could be the smoking gun you're looking for…"

Put your own mushroom-spotting abilities to the test by navigating your way through this mushroom maze from top-left to bottom-right as quickly as you can. You may move from a mushroom to any other mushroom in its row or column, providing that mushroom is either the same type or contains the same number of spots. What is the minimum number of steps required to move from the start to the finish?

#  A GAME OF CHESS

It's late in the day now, but Heather resolves to see Judith right away in light of what she now knows. Last time they spoke briefly, and Judith played down the significance of her argument with Sam. This time Heather needs to get a watertight alibi from Judith, if she has one. She knows the chess and bridge club are meeting tonight at the village hall and wagers that Judith will be there, since Carol told her previously that Judith is a big fan.

The gamble pays off as, on arrival, Heather sees Judith bent over a chessboard, trying to work something out. She frowns as Heather walks over and greets her with the words, "You broke my concentration – thanks!"

Heather apologises and says she needs to ask her some more questions. She explains some potentially incriminating evidence has come to light and that they need to talk about it urgently.

"Is this what my life's come to?" asks Judith with a sigh, before wearily adding: "When I was growing up, I used to have great plans for the future. I was going to write a best-selling novel, become famous, marry someone handsome and successful and now I'm sitting here playing chess and I'm also a suspect in a murder investigation. What a combination!"

Heather has limited sympathy for her – no-one's life turns out how they plan it except in some soporific movies – and says she really does need to talk to her urgently. Judith says that, as Heather broke her concentration, the least she can do is to first assist her in solving this chess puzzle. Each letter from A to E represents a different chess piece: a queen, a knight, a bishop, a king and a rook in some order. The numbers on some squares indicate the number of pieces that can attack that square using standard chess rules. Use this information to help you solve the puzzle logically.

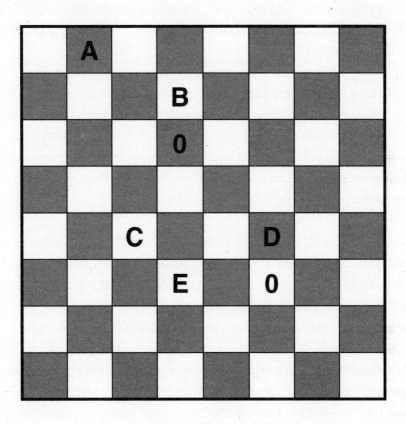

A =

B =

C =

D =

E =

# 48 A BRIDGE TOO FAR

Judith is thankful for the help Heather has offered, and decides to push her luck:

"Would you mind taking a look at this one too? I can't quite see how to get started."

Heather is uncertain – she is here on serious police business, after all. If Judith is guilty and knows why Heather's here, she's acting remarkably casually. However, Heather finds a blank grid irresistible – it just cries out to be filled in. Solving puzzles and solving crimes aren't that different, really, so she vaguely justifies it to herself as helping keep her skills sharp.

To solve the bridge puzzle, you must place 25 unique letter/symbol combinations into the grid once each. They are the A,2,3,4 and 5 of each of the four suits (clubs, diamonds, hearts and spades) and also NT for 'no trumps'. In each row and column there must be one of each card value (A,2,3,4,5) and one of each symbol (club, diamond, heart, spade and NT). Use the cross-off chart to keep track of the 25 combinations. Some information has been placed in the grid to get you started.

| | | | | ♣ |
|---|---|---|---|---|
| | ♣ | | ♦ | |
| 4 | | | A | |
| ♦ | NT | | | 3 |
| | ♥ | 2♣ | | |

| | ♣ | ♦ | ♥ | ♠ | NT |
|---|---|---|---|---|---|
| A | | | | | |
| 2 | | | | | |
| 3 | | | | | |
| 4 | | | | | |
| 5 | | | | | |

**MIXED SUCCESS**

Satisfied with the help provided, Judith finally starts talking. Having focused on Sam previously, Heather asks her first about her relationship with Dennis. Judith says she knew him through the foraging society of course, but not socially and they didn't have much contact with each other. It seems clear that Judith's contact with Dennis had been minimal, which possibly counts in her favour now Heather knows the cases are surely linked. She therefore moves on swiftly to ask her again about Sam and that argument. Judith elaborates that, truth be told, they did argue rather a lot:

"I'd spotted a pattern of treachery on his part, if that's not too strong a word. We used to be annual champions in the mixed doubles at Upper Gorsetown Lawn Tennis Club. We won the event together for several years." She then pauses, and smiles wistfully, clearly recalling with considerable nostalgia highlights of their time together on court. She then giggles and adds, "This one time, on match point, our opponents tried to cheat. I hit a shot plumb on the baseline and when they called it out, quick as a flash my Sam, erm, I mean Sam, said, 'If you called it long then you called it wrong.' We replayed the point and won it, and the tournament. Happy times!" She pauses, her face starts to sour, and then she says through what Heather fancies are gritted teeth, "Then he unceremoniously dumped me as his partner for his wife. Now, fair enough, she probably begged him to play with her, but Sandy's not exactly gifted on the court, or indeed at anything, come to think of it! Not the brightest crayon in the box, that one. They barely won a match playing together whereas we used to win with ease. Well, that got my back up and led to an argument. Since then our relationship hasn't been what it was, so when I found out he'd been promising someone else his committee vote at the foraging society, I had more than a few choice words for him, shall we say."

"However, despite that row the other day, I'm very happy in a new relationship with a wonderful man and all I can do is emphasise again that I wouldn't kill one man over an argument, let alone him and a friend of his who I barely know! I assume you are looking for one person in connection with both murders?"

Heather thinks about this for a minute. No-one outside of the police knows that both deaths are being treated as murder, nor the link that has been established by the same type of mushroom being used to poison them both. This is a bit suspicious.

"Why do you think they are connected?" Heather enquires.

"Well, only that you have come to see me again, so I assume you have some new information, and you did just ask me about Dennis too!" Judith replies.

"Hmm… I suppose that makes sense!" muses Heather. "You mention being happy with your new partner – what is his name?"

Solve this puzzle to reveal the name of Judith's new partner, which will be revealed along the highlighted diagonal. You must place each of the six letters C, E, N, O, R, T once in each row, column and 3x2 bold-outlined box.

| | | | | | |
|---|---|---|---|---|---|
| | | R | | | T |
| | | | R | | C |
| O | | | T | | |
| | | C | | | O |
| R | | T | | | |
| N | | | E | | |

# 50 TIMES TABLE

Heather now plays her trump card, asking Judith why someone suspects her of murder enough to have provided a tip off to the police asking them to search her bins. Heather goes on to inform Judith that they did just that and have found what they believe to be poisonous mushrooms, pending the results of some tests. On hearing the news, all the blood suddenly drains from Judith's face, and she starts stuttering.

"I… I've… no idea why, or who that could be. I haven't even cooked with mushrooms recently, so anything in my bin must have been planted there by someone who wants me to take the fall for this. Maybe I'm an easy target as people know about the friction between me and Sam. But… it's… it's nothing to do with me!"

Heather asks Judith if she has any enemies who might want to implicate her. Judith thinks for a second and says no, not really, she has friction with a few people in the foraging society, such as Carol, but nothing of note. Heather asks her to think carefully about her denial, but Judith sticks to her line, insisting that if there were poisonous mushrooms in her rubbish, they were placed there by the perpetrator of the crime.

Heather informs Judith that given the seriousness of the matter she will need to provide an alibi as to her whereabouts the evening before Dennis's body was found, which was also the evening when Sam collapsed and was taken to hospital before dying. Judith states that she was with Connor the whole time. They were on a date at a restaurant in nearby Lower Gorsetown before spending the night together.

Judith has regained her composure by now, and goes on to say how amazing Connor is and waxes lyrical about him. Solve this puzzle to find out the number of times his name is mentioned. To do so, find the word 'CONNOR' as many times as you can by moving from letter to letter horizontally or vertically one letter at a time in the grid below.

# SILENT PARTNER

Heather gets Connor's address from Judith, and goes to see him. It's dark outside now, and the surrounding woodland looks strangely sinister. She hears a loud sneeze, so she knows someone's home.

She knocks on the door, and a man answers.

"Connor, I presume?"

He nods, and ushers her in with a sweep of his arm. Clearly a man of few words. However, he is a man of a lot of sneezes, and does so five times in a row, with no tissue in sight. "Did the pandemic never happen?" Heather mutters, loud enough that Connor hears her and replies in monosyllabic fashion "Hay fever!" Heather is not overly reassured.

Once inside, Heather asks him where he was on the evening in question, and he tells the same story Judith did, using as few words as he can: he had picked Judith up at around 6pm and then taken her to a restaurant for a nice meal. They had then returned to his house and spent the night together. He shows Heather the receipt from the restaurant they ate at to prove he is telling the truth. Heather examines it carefully – everything seems to check out.

Satisfied with the alibi, and realising talking to Connor is like trying to get blood out of a stone, Heather turns to leave. As she does so, Connor says quietly, "It would be an act of great folly, detective, to suspect my dear Judith of the most trivial of crimes, let alone the most serious." This struck Heather as a slightly unusual thing to say, and particularly so given, until then at least, he seemed to have an aversion to speaking.

Speaking of unusual, as she looks at the receipt again, Heather notices that the restaurant has a very distinctive logo. By examining it, can you work out the restaurant's name?

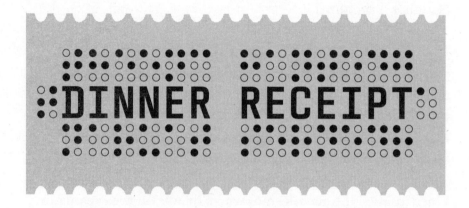

# 52 HOME, SWEET HOME

It's the weekend, and Heather wakes up thinking about the case. It's hard not to when her main suspects so far seem to have credible alibis, and her boss keeps asking her if she's solved the case yet. "No pressure, then!" she says to herself.

She decides to drive to see her parents for the first time since she moved to Ivyville. After such a busy week investigating the two likely murders, she needs some time to rest and mull things over.

Not being a fan of sat navs ever since one tried to take her off the edge of a cliff once, she goes old school and takes out a trusty map. She'd once had to explain to her niece what one of those was. Having not had time to explore the neighbouring areas since starting the job, Heather decides to visit each of the places shown on the map below, en route to her parents.

Can you help Heather work out the shortest route between Ivyville and the town where her parents live, Pebbleston, whilst visiting each of the other locations once along the way? The diagram below is not drawn to scale. The numbers in circles represent the distance in miles between each pair of locations joined by a line.

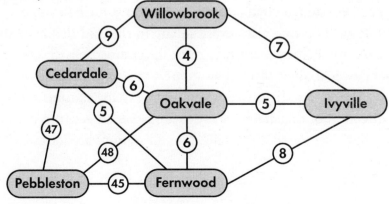

# 53 NIGHT TRAIN

When she reaches Pebbleston, Heather is reassured to experience all the familiar sights and sounds of home. She always finds it comforting returning to this little oasis of calm.

Her mother, Mary, greets her as her car enters the driveway. She has clearly been waiting for her. Heather enquires as to where her dad is, as it's unusual for him not to also come and say hello straightaway. They'd spent ages when she lived at home asking her when she was going to fly the nest, and then when she did they kept on asking when she was going to come back and visit them.

"Oh, I can't get him off those blasted trains, dear! Ever since he took up the hobby he's been obsessed, I tell you. He's playing with the flipping things morning, noon and night. You'll have to go and prise him off them I'm afraid!"

Heather nods, and goes to the garage which is very much her dad's domain. She knocks on the door, and enters. Sure enough she sees her dad tinkering with his impressive train set.

Can you recreate the shape of the train track and locate all the stations her dad has sited around it? The track forms a single continuous loop that visits every square in the grid that is neither a station nor a clue square. The track never crosses itself, and it either passes straight through a square or turns at right angles in it. Cells containing arrows tell you how many stations are in the direction of that arrow. Stations are never adjacent to each other, but may touch diagonally. Not all stations are indicated by arrows.

| | | | | | | | |
|---|---|---|---|---|---|---|---|
| | | | | | | | |
| | | | | | | | 2↓ |
| | | | | | | | |
| | | | | 2↑ | | | |
| | | | | | | ←2 | |
| 2↑ | | | | | | | |
| | | | | | | | |
| | | | →2 | | | | |

# (54) TRAIN OF THOUGHT

Heather's dad, Colin, looks up from his trains and gives her a beaming smile.

"Ah, hello love. I lost track of time! Something always needs fixing with these trains; one of them always seems to be about to break down. Just like the real thing, right?" Heather simpers as her father laughs out loud.

Mary wanders into the room, and asks Heather how the new job is going. Whilst she doesn't usually talk about her work, she decides to recount the details of the case to them, and what her enquiries have turned up so far. She confesses she doesn't feel too confident about cracking the case: her main suspects for either one or both murders, Jeremy and Gemma, seem to have reasonable alibis, whilst Judith, who had argued so publicly with Sam, also appears to have a credible alibi.

She wonders out loud who Father Stibley was surprised to see at confession, and who the mystery third person in the pub argument was.

"That mysterious person in the pub is who you need to identify, sure as eggs are eggs," her mother says. Heather nods, and explains that she had asked at the pub if they knew who it was, and no-one did. Sam's widow also wasn't able to help.

"From what you say, you only spoke to his wife once, right after he died. Maybe it's worth speaking to her again, and see if you can find out if there was anyone apart from this Judith who might have had a grudge against him. She'll have had time to think about what happened by now. Or perhaps he kept a diary that could give you some clues as to what he was doing in the days before he died."

Heather thanks them for the wise counsel, then spends the rest of the weekend trying not to think too much about work, and enjoys passing the time in familiar ways, playing various card games and board games. She soon regresses to childhood and gets just as competitive with her dad as they always used to when she was a youngster. She is therefore very pleased when she beats his initial seven-letter word with an eight-letter word of her own in the board game shown below. Can you work out the eight-letter word that Heather played using all the letters shown around the grid below? Since Heather has seven letters to use, her answer must intersect the word her dad played somewhere on the grid.

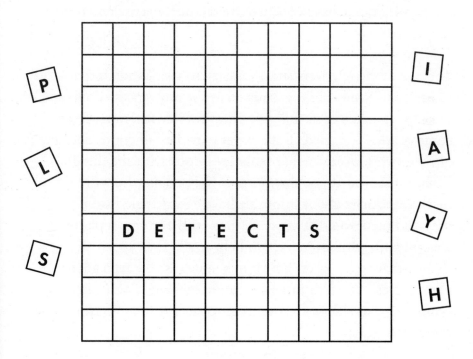

#  DEAR DIARY

Back home, and feeling refreshed after seeing her parents, Heather heads straight over to see Sandy Turner on Monday morning. En route she finds out that the mushrooms found in Judith's rubbish bin have been confirmed as fool's funnel. She scratches her head. Judith has a watertight alibi – she's even seen the receipt of her meal with Connor. Either there is very clever deception at play here, or the murderer has inadvertently shown their hand, perhaps through panic, and is trying to distract Heather. She has plenty to think about, but right now has to concentrate on driving: she has to slam on the brakes as she realises that a deer is crossing the road. Such are the perils of the countryside. She's lost count of the number of times she's seen a warning sign relating to animals crossing the road and not seen one; typically she has now encountered one where there is no sign to be seen!

The rest of the relatively short journey to visit Sandy is thankfully uneventful. Sandy looks exhausted as she answers the door, and she explains she's been suffering from terrible insomnia since Sam's death. "I've tried all the usual remedies, of course, but none of them work. And I refuse tablets – I don't trust the things. It's become clear to me that none of the people who write these incessant articles about insomnia have ever actually had it. If they had they wouldn't make all those silly recommendations… a warm bath with lavender? No help at all! Then I read all these articles telling you how important it is you get a good night's sleep… well, it just adds to the pressure, doesn't it?" As sympathetic as she is, Heather tries to steer the conversation to the matter at hand.

She knows Sandy has been informed that the fatal mushrooms her husband consumed were fool's funnel, but she doesn't yet know that Dennis had also ingested the same mushrooms. When Heather tells her this, Sandy is stunned:

"Goodness me. Everyone told me he was stabbed! So someone deliberately poisoned my husband *and* Dennis? But who would do such a thing, and why?"

"That's exactly what we are trying to establish," replies Heather, before adding: "Rest assured we're doing all we can, Mrs. Turner, and enquiries are ongoing." It was police-speak, but also completely true.

"Last time we spoke you knew he had been out picking mushrooms during the day, but didn't know he'd been at the pub with Dennis in the afternoon where they argued with someone else. I really need to identify who that other person was. Did Sam keep a diary of some sort, or use a planner where he might have written down a 'to do' list for the day? It's important you think carefully as anything we find may well help us piece together what happened."

Sandy thinks for a while and then tells Heather that whilst he didn't keep a diary, he did use the planner on his laptop to keep a log of his movements. She says Heather is welcome to go up to his study with her and look there. The only problem is that he never shared his password.

They open the laptop, and Sandy tries a couple of guesses, but has no luck: unlike a certain percentage of the population, his password is not 'password123'. Then Heather spies a piece of paper stuck to the wall above Sam's desk that says 'Remind me' on it very faintly, and also contains what appears to be a puzzle. She thinks there's a chance that this is a password reminder that Sam has created for himself. She deduces that she will need to shift each letter of 'SMILES' along the alphabet by the amount indicated by one of the numbers. For instance, 'A' shifted 11 places would become 'L', whilst 'Z' shifted one place would become 'A', and so on.

She applies this method, using each number once to shift the letters of 'SMILES' in turn to create a common word. Can you do likewise, working out which number pairs with each letter to shift it the correct number of positions in the alphabet to create the password?

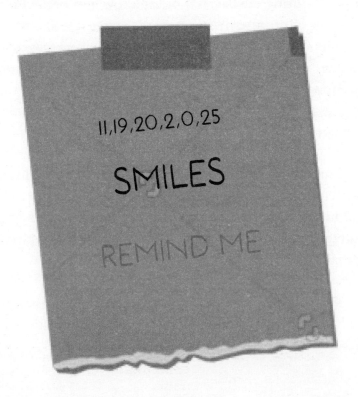

# 56 ON SCHEDULE

Heather enters what she thinks must be the password, and is rewarded by the system loading. She now has access to Sam's files. Clicking around the desktop, she soon finds the planner, and poignantly sees that Sam had plans for today, which he will never fulfil. She scrolls back to look at what Sam had planned for that fateful day.

However, it appears that he had added an additional layer of security to scramble the itinerary for the day in question. Can you work out what Sam's schedule was?

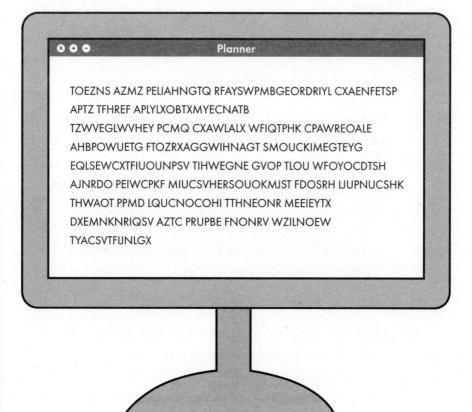

```
                                    Planner

    TOEZNS AZMZ PELIAHNGTQ RFAYSWPMBGEORDRIYL CXAENFETSP
    APTZ TFHREF APLYLXOBTXMYECNATB
    TZWVEGLWVHEY PCMQ CXAWLALX WFIQTPHK CPAWREOALE
    AHBPOWUETG FTOZRXAGGWIHNAGT SMOUCKIMEGTEYG
    EQLSEWCXTFIUOUNPSV TIHWEGNE GVOP TLOU WFOYOCDTSH
    AJNRDO PEIWCPKF MIUCSVHERSOUOKMJST FDOSRH LJUPNUCSHK
    THWAOT PPMD LQUCNOCOHI TTHNEONR MEEIEYTX
    DXEMNKNRIQSV AZTC PRUPBE FNONRV WZILNOEW
    TYACSVTFIJNLGX
```

# GRUDGE MATCH

Heather is both pleased and disappointed. Pleased, because she now has a timeline for some of Sam's movements. In particular, she can see he ate lunch at around 2pm using the mushrooms he had foraged. This rules out him accidentally poisoning himself with fool's funnel as he must have ingested them later in the day for the timescales of his symptoms and death to fit. Disappointed, because Sam didn't have anything scheduled for early evening which is when she believes the poisoning must have happened. Anything he did then must have been impromptu, or at least something he didn't want to record on paper. Heather was hoping for a helping hand from the dead. After all, her hitherto best suspects for the murders, Jeremy, Gemma and Judith, all had alibis that put them out of action from about the time she surmised the two victims had ingested the mushrooms, or at least were on the very edge of plausibility.

Heather had asked Sandy when they first spoke if she knew who he could have been with at the pub in addition to Dennis, but she had no idea. So instead she asks if there is anyone who could have had a grudge against Sam. Sandy thinks for a while, and says that most people got on well with Sam. She mentions Judith, and that she had really riled Sam on several occasions. Heather says that she has spoken on multiple occasions to Judith, and is there anyone else she can think of?

After some thought, Sandy says: "Well, I suppose there is always Mo. Mo Ali, that is. She was at school with Sam and he played a prank on her once and embarrassed her in front of the class. That unfortunately led to her being teased for years by the other students. She dropped her diary and he'd photocopied the worst bits for a laugh and put them up around the school. Not his finest moment, but it was a schoolboy prank. She hated him for it and even got her brother to beat him up once, I believe. Come to think of it, she didn't much like Dennis either as he always defended Sam."

"And do you know if Sam has seen this Mo Ali lately?"

"Well, she lives fairly close to us so we occasionally ran into each other in town and it was always awkward. She gave him daggers. I'm not aware of any direct contact of late, but Sam is quite private so I suppose it's possible; I wouldn't really know. Maybe Mo had been biding her time and suddenly struck all these years later? It sounds a bit far-fetched but hell hath no fury, as they say…"

There is clearly enough here that Heather needs to speak to Mo. She is about to call the station to get Mo's address, when Sandy says "Oh, there's no need, I think Sam had it written down somewhere… hold on a second…" which strikes Heather as odd.

Sandy gives Heather a piece of paper and says, "Here's a diagram showing the eight houses in the road in which Mo lives. As you'll see, they are arranged in quite singular fashion and there is no rhyme nor reason to the house numbers, as far as I can tell. Mo's house number is the sum of the digits in the squares that contain stars. You'll just need to place digits from 1-9 in each row and column that sum to the house numbers shown, ensuring you don't repeat a number in a row or column. Oh and one final thing – the grey squares must contain even numbers."

Heather wishes she'd just called the station – it would have been simpler. However, she can't resist tackling the puzzle and thus finding Mo's house number. What is it?

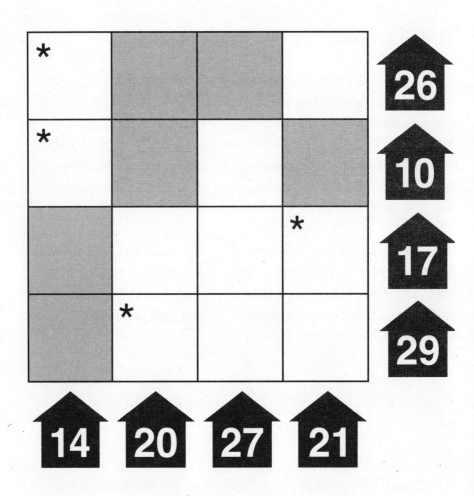

# 58 PRINT PREVIEW

There are lots of files on the desk in Sam's study. Heather starts moving them around, and her eyes alight on a piece of paper. Superficially it appears to relate to mushroom picking, but it is formatted unusually, and Heather's keen eyes spot another message. Can you find it?

- KNOWLEDGE IS
- ESSENTIAL WHEN
  YOU ARE
- ENSURING YOU ONLY
- PICK EDIBLE MUSHROOMS.
- HUBRIS CAN BE
- EXTREMELY DANGEROUS
  SO BE SURE
  TO CHECK AND
- RECHECK WHAT
  YOU PICK.
- SOME USEFUL
- WORDS OF WISDOM:
- YOU ARE ONLY
- EVER ONE
- ERRONEOUSLY PICKED
  MUSHROOM FROM
  DEATH. THAT'S
  A VERY SOBERING
- THOUGHT INDEED.

# 59 LOCATION, LOCATION, LOCATION

"Who do you think that might be about?" Heather asks Sandy.

"I imagine it could be about Judith – as you know she was very angry when she realised Sam had promised his vote to Clara for secretary, as well as her, in the upcoming foraging society elections. Not something I approved of, I hasten to add, but Sam always was a bit of a political animal and that's how things work in that world, isn't it? You scratch my back and I may or may not scratch yours."

Heather thought there seemed to be a million miles between the Upper Gorsetown foraging society and the corridors of power in Westminster, but perhaps any sniff of power is enough to make people do questionable things.

"Or I suppose it *could* be Mo – you know, if she had been in touch recently threatening Sam or something and I didn't know about it?"

Heather scribbles this all down in her notepad, before her eyes alight on a curious piece of text on the reverse of the 'keep her sweet' note.

Can you work out what it says?

L N I R E N N

ƆO S H E M I

C I R T C U N

A T O W O L E

# SAFE CODE

Heather notes this down in her pad. How mysterious! She asks Sandy if she can shed any light on it, but she shakes her head and says she doesn't have the faintest idea what it could mean, before adding:

"There is a safe in the bedroom that Sam always kept locked. I never look in there but I suppose you might find something in it that could help you."

They move to the bedroom, and Heather is shown the safe.

"You need to press four buttons in order to open the safe," Sandy says. "I never use it enough to remember which ones, so Sam gave me a hint if I ever needed it. Hold on a minute!"

Sandy rummages around for a while, then comes back and shows Heather a crumpled piece of paper, and says:

"This diagram represents a sequence in which all 25 buttons on the safe have been pressed once each, ending on the square marked 'X'. To open the safe, you need to work out which were the first four buttons in the sequence of 25 to be pressed, then push the corresponding buttons on the real safe."

Can you work out which were the first four buttons to be pressed and therefore will open the real-life safe? Arrows show which button was pressed next. For instance, the 2↓ at the top-left of the grid means that the button two-below it was next to be pressed after that one.

| | | | | |
|---|---|---|---|---|
| 2↓ | 2↓ | 2← | 3↓ | 3↓ |
| 1→ | X | 3↓ | 1→ | 3↓ |
| 1↓ | 3→ | 2↑ | 1↑ | 2← |
| 3↗ | 3↑ | 2↑ | 1↑ | 1↙ |
| 3↑ | 1← | 1↖ | 2← | 4↑ |

# 61 POISON PEN LETTER

Inside the safe are the usual valuables you'd expect, such as a passport and a wad of banknotes for an emergency. There are also several pieces of paper in there.

Heather takes a look at the first of these, which is dated just a few days before Sam died. It appears to be a poison pen letter of some sort. Can you take one letter from each row to deduce what it threatens?

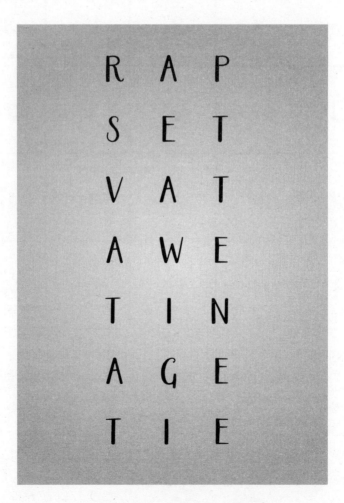

# IN THE MONEY

Sandy lets out a little gasp as Heather reveals the contents of the poison pen letter. It seems clear that Sam was being blackmailed or threatened – but by whom, and why?

Intrigued, Heather looks at the next document, which is a recent bank statement.

It seems to be one that Sam has printed off, but not before he has encoded the 'credit/debit' and 'details' columns. Can you crack the code to reveal a surprising transfer?

| Date | Amount (£) | Credit/debit | Details |
|---|---|---|---|
| Xx/xx/xxxx | 5.00 | C2 C14 V2 C3 V3 C16 | V3 C11 C16 V2 C14 V2 C15 C16 |
| Xx/xx/xxxx | 1,100 | C3 V2 C1 V3 C16 | C10 V4 C14 C16 C5 V1 C5 V2 C12 V1 C20 C10 V2 C11 C16 |
| Xx/xx/xxxx | 10,000 | C2 C14 V2 C3 V3 C16 | C4 C14 V4 C10 C3 V2 C11 C11 V3 C15 C1 V1 C8 V2 C14 |

# THREATENING BEHAVIOUR

Why had one of the two dead men, Dennis Baker, recently given the other dead man, Sam Turner, a large sum of money? Heather hadn't been expecting that. Unfortunately Sandy could shed no light on it either and said she knew nothing about it. It seems to Heather that Sam was keeping a lot from his wife, or... was Sandy a little too unaware of what was going on? Heather wonders if she should be suspicious of Sandy after all, although surely she wouldn't have given Heather access to the safe if she had anything to hide. Would she? Whatever the truth, her knowledge of her husband's life was proving about as useful as the proverbial chocolate teapot.

Heather thumbs through the other bits of paper in the safe, and doesn't see anything else of note. One of the pieces of paper is completely blank apart from the word 'stamps' written at the top, which strikes Heather as odd.

"Stamps – what do you think that means?" she muses aloud.

"Aha, now that I can help with!" says Sandy. "Sam is... was... a bit of a stamp collector, and he uses a little UV device to display the phosphor bands on various stamps to help ascertain their value. Hold on a sec..."

Sandy goes into another room and Heather hears the sound of boxes being moved around. In short order she comes back with a UV light and shines it over the page. As if by magic, the following text appears, glowing in a ghostly shade of bluish-purple:

Heather looks at the text and frowns for a minute – can you work out what it means?

# 64 FOOD FOR THOUGHT

"Who could this Moira be?" Heather asks.

Sandy thinks for a second and then says, "Ah – I believe 'Mo' is short for 'Moira' – it must be Moira Ali, who I just told you about! As I say, she hated Sam and disliked Dennis too. You've got her address – you should go and see her!"

With all the documents in the safe now having been looked at, and a new lead to look into, Heather leaves, satisfied with a very productive visit.

En route to visit Moira Ali, her stomach rumbles and she stops at a shop for some necessary provisions. Heather buys at least one of each of the following items:

45p

59p

88p

Heather spends £3.98 in total.
How many of each item did she buy?

# 65 A SHAKY START

"I would feel guilty eating three chocolate bars," she says to the shopkeeper, "but have you seen the size of them these days? Talk about shrinkflation. These are what used to be called fun size when I was growing up!"

Heather returns to her car, and having wolfed down the snacks in short order, she feels re-energised and completes the shortish journey to visit Moira in the nearby town where she lives.

She rings the bell and a lady answers the door, looking very twitchy.

"Hello, are you Moira Ali?" Heather enquires. The lady nods.

"My name's Detective Heather Vintner. Can I come in please?"

Moira looks taken aback and ushers Heather inside the house, then closes the door.

"Can I get you a tea or coffee?" she asks. Heather says a glass of water will be fine. Moira fills a glass and then sets it down on the table, her hand shaking slightly. She fills another glass for herself.

"I'm awfully sorry, I always get nervous around the police although I have nothing to hide. I don't know why. When I see a police car drive past me on the street I'm always anxious they'll stop and pull me over for something. It's silly, I know. I'm the same in shops: when I leave I'm always worried those infernal detectors at the exits will start beeping and I'll be accused of stealing something, even though I've never taken anything in my life."

Heather tries to reassure her, which is a little difficult when she is about to ask her if she has killed two men. She sits down at the table, and asks Moira to do the same.

Heather notices that Moira is gulping down her water, presumably due to nerves.

Moira is drinking from a glass that she filled with 300ml of water. She drank a third of the water on her first gulp, then half of what was left on the second gulp, followed by 70% of what was then left on her third gulp. How much water is still in the glass?

#  IDENTITY CRISIS

"I'm here to talk to you about the murder of Sam Turner," Heather says.

Moira shivers at the mention of Sam's name, and says that she had heard about the shocking events in Upper Gorsetown on the news.

"It's awful isn't it? Just ghastly. How can I help you, detective?"

Heather asks her when she last saw Sam.

"It must be a month or so ago. I don't like to speak ill of the dead, but he wasn't a very nice man. I was at school with him. He played a prank on me that was quite unforgivable – ruined my whole school experience, it did. Well of course he's grown up a lot since then, but a leopard never changes its spots, does it?"

"And when you saw him a month ago, how were things?"

"Well, I would like to be the bigger person, but I have to be honest and say I always gave him a few choice words or a bit of an angry stare when our paths crossed. I have never forgotten what he did. But that doesn't mean I wanted the man dead!"

Heather shows her the note she had found in Sam's safe that read: "MOIRA, WHY NOW? NO GOOD CAN COME OF THIS" and asks her to comment.

Moira scratches her head, and says she has no idea why he would have a note that mentioned her. If he thought she had been threatening him for some reason, it must be a case of mistaken identity. Moira said that she did occasionally get confused for other people as she has quite a generic look.

Can you work out which one of these faces matches that of the real Moira exactly?

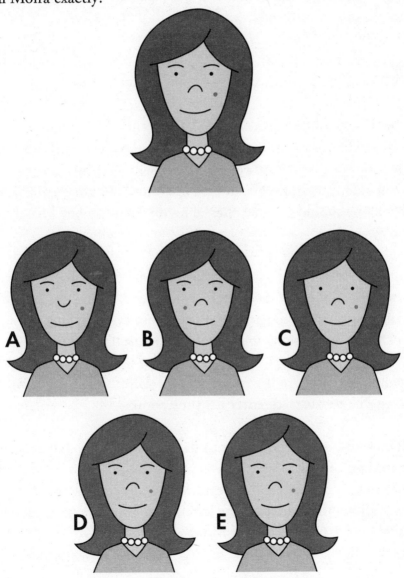

#  INNOCENT PARTY

Moira then says several times that she is innocent, and can't provide any further help. Heather doesn't think this is the most convincing defence. Could Moira be shaking simply because she does have something to hide? Heather wants to hear what Moira has to say about Dennis.

"And, can I ask, did you know Dennis Baker? If you know Sam is dead then I'm sure you've heard that Dennis is also?"

Moira nods and says: "Yes, I was sorry to hear about that, of course. He was good friends with Sam, wasn't he? I wasn't a fan of Dennis, but then I didn't know him well at all. I imagine it's not a coincidence that they both died at around the same time. And that alone should rule me out: I'd hardly kill someone I barely knew, would I?"

Heather realises that Moira is trying as best as she can to distance herself from the pair. She needs to find out if Moira has an alibi that covers her for the period of time from early evening through to Dennis' body being found stabbed the next morning.

Moira provides herself with an alibi by claiming she was at work. Solve this puzzle to discover her profession.

In each row, write the answer to the crossword clue that appears at the end of that row. Once you have solved the puzzle correctly, the same four words will appear horizontally in the rows and vertically in the columns. The letters in the squares that are numbered 1-6 will spell out Moira's job.

| | | | 1 |
|---|---|---|---|
| | 3 | 6 | |
| | | 2 | 5 |
| | | | 4 |

Stated

Unit of land area

Metallic element

Depression in a surface

# 68 THE GRAVEYARD SHIFT

Moira says that she works at a hospital and was on call from around 6pm to 6am on the day in question, so she can prove that she couldn't have been the murderer.

Heather asks for the name of the hospital so that she can head straight over there and verify that Moira was indeed on shift when she says she was. Moira duly provides the name, and tells Heather to ask for Consultant Carter when she gets there.

Solve these cryptic crossword clues to reveal the name of the hospital. You must use each of the letters shown once to create your six answers, so cross them off as you use them.

1) At butcher's, repositioned vegetarian dish (10)

| 1 | 2 | 3 | 4 | 5 | 6 | 7 | 8 | 9 | 10 |
|---|---|---|---|---|---|---|---|---|----|
|   |   |   |   |   |   |   |   |   |    |

2) Sole voter sorted for US President (9)

| 11 | 12 | 13 | 14 | 15 | 16 | 17 | 18 | 19 |
|----|----|----|----|----|----|----|----|----|
|    |    |    |    |    |    |    |    |    |

3) Excuse average fellow (6)

| 20 | 21 | 22 | 23 | 24 | 25 |
|----|----|----|----|----|----|
|    |    |    |    |    |    |

4) Lean monarch is pensive (8)

| 26 | 27 | 28 | 29 | 30 | 31 | 32 | 33 |
|----|----|----|----|----|----|----|----|
|    |    |    |    |    |    |    |    |

5) Fruit hidden in cheap ricotta (7)

| 34 | 35 | 36 | 37 | 38 | 39 | 40 |
|----|----|----|----|----|----|----|
|    |    |    |    |    |    |    |

6) Still a monster (4)

| 41 | 42 | 43 | 44 |
|----|----|----|----|
|    |    |    |    |

| A | A | A | B | C | C | D | E | E | E | E |
|---|---|---|---|---|---|---|---|---|---|---|
| G | H | H | I | I | I | I | K | L | N | N |
| N | O | O | O | O | P | P | R | R | R | R |
| S | S | T | T | T | T | T | T | U | V | Y |

Once you have solved the clues, the following letters will reveal the name of the hospital:

5, 39, 3, 29, 8, 41   33, 7, 32, 42, 2, 21, 18

# 69 A CHANGE OF DIRECTION

At the hospital Heather tries to find Moira's boss, Consultant Carter. Unfortunately, like many hospitals, getting lost is easy, whilst finding where you want to go is hard.

Heather goes to reception and asks for help. Moira has told her that she specialises in diet, so she asks the receptionist to point her to the relevant department.

The receptionist prints out the following list of departments and locations. Unfortunately the printer has malfunctioned and swapped around two pairs of letters. Can you crack the code, identify the departments and therefore work out where Heather needs to go to find Consultant Carter?

**EBSTOTRACS**
FARST FLEER, GROON ZENO
**CRATACIL CIRO**
SOCEND FLEER, ROD ZENO
**HIOMITELEGY**
THARD FLEER, YOLLEW ZENO
**DAOTOTACS**
SOCEND FLEER, GROON ZENO
**NOPHRELEGY**
FARST FLEER, YOLLEW ZENO
**CIRDAELEGY**
THARD FLEER, GROON ZENO
**NOENITIL**
SOCEND FLEER, YOLLEW ZENO

# HOSPITAL PASS

Heather uses the directions she has been given to locate the correct department, and is slightly out of breath when she gets there. "Typical that it was on the second floor!" she says to herself. She used to hate the annual 'bleep' test back when she'd had to do it.

She knocks on Consultant Carter's door, and a voice says "Come in."

Heather enters and introduces herself. She feels self-conscious as the consultant looks at her, hoping that he isn't going to offer her any dietary advice. She knew she shouldn't have eaten all those chocolate bars over the last few years but when they taste so good the willpower required not to yield to temptation is difficult to come by!

Luckily the consultant settles for the straightforward "How can I help you, detective?"

Heather explains that she needs to know if Moira Ali was working when she said she was. The consultant tilts his head quizzically, and explains that he has a log of all the different people working in the department and their shift patterns.

"Unfortunately it's a little complicated – you know what the bureaucracy is like in a place like this!" he says enigmatically.

He pulls out a grid for the relevant date that has the names of various workers around the edge, together with a record of the hours they worked, the room number they were based in and the name of their supervisor for that date.

"All I need to know is whether Moira Ali was working from 6pm to 6am or not, Consultant Carter. This looks a little convoluted," protests Heather.

Consultant Carter shrugs and says, "As I say, detective… bureaucracy." He then grins like a Cheshire cat. "But rest assured, everything you need to know is here, but I'm afraid you are going to have to work through it all systematically to find your answer!"

Is Moira telling the truth? Use the clues provided, together with the cross-referencing chart, to work out the shift each person in dietetics worked, the room they were in and the name of their supervisor.

## CLUES

– Dominic worked from a room whose number is two greater than the room the person supervised by Dr. Hawthorne was based in.

– The person supervised by Dr. Chen worked in a room whose number is neither one greater nor one lower than the room used by the person who finished their shift at 6am.

– The person whose shift started at 4pm was based in room 3.

– Isabella did not start work at 3pm. Whoever did start at that time was not based in room 1.

– The person who started their shift at 6pm worked from the room whose number is one greater than Dominic's room.

– Moira's supervisor was Dr. Nguyen.

|  | Supervisor | | | | Room Number | | | | Hours worked | | | |
|---|---|---|---|---|---|---|---|---|---|---|---|---|
|  | Dr. Chen | Dr. Hawthorne | Dr. Nguyen | Dr. Ramirez | 1 | 2 | 3 | 4 | 3pm-3am | 4pm-4am | 5pm-5am | 6pm-6am |
| **Employee** Dominic |  |  |  |  |  |  |  |  |  |  |  |  |
| Isabella |  |  |  |  |  |  |  |  |  |  |  |  |
| Janice |  |  |  |  |  |  |  |  |  |  |  |  |
| Moira |  |  |  |  |  |  |  |  |  |  |  |  |
| **Hours worked** 3pm-3am |  |  |  |  |  |  |  |  |
| 4pm-4am |  |  |  |  |  |  |  |  |
| 5pm-5am |  |  |  |  |  |  |  |  |
| 6pm-6am |  |  |  |  |  |  |  |  |
| **Room Number** 1 |  |  |  |  |
| 2 |  |  |  |  |
| 3 |  |  |  |  |
| 4 |  |  |  |  |

| Employee | Hours worked | Room Number | Supervisor |
|---|---|---|---|
| Dominic |  |  |  |
| Isabella |  |  |  |
| Janice |  |  |  |
| Moira |  |  |  |

# DEAD END

It's there in black-and-white: Moira was working when both men were poisoned and when Dennis was found stabbed. Heather is therefore satisfied that Moira is innocent as her alibi appears unimpeachable. But this doesn't explain why Sam had a note mentioning her name.

Heather heads home to rest after a long day, making a quick detour on the way to visit Sandy and update her as a matter of courtesy. Sandy thanks her, and says that she did consider Moira to be something of a long shot.

"Keep me in the loop, please," she says as Heather leaves a few minutes later. Heather promises to do so.

Can you work out the shape of the loop in the following puzzle? The loop visits every square in the grid, and either passes straight through a square or turns at right angles in it. The loop cannot cross itself.

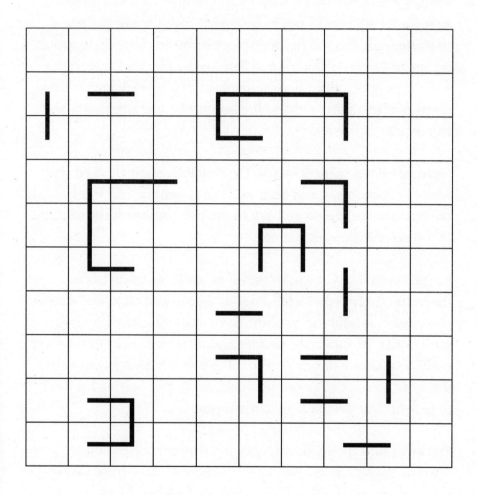

**THREE'S A CROWD**

It's a beautiful morning with sun streaming through the windows, and Heather wakes up determined to make progress after Moira Ali turned out to be a dead end. One of the few concrete leads she still has to explore is the fact that there was an argument between Dennis and Sam in the pub and that there was a mysterious third person involved that no-one knew. That seems odd in a fairly tight-knit community, and suggests it was an outsider. But who?

Heather knows there is no CCTV available: she'd checked that with Gus previously and been told the system he had in place is broken. She decides to go back to the pub and see if she can find anyone else with information.

As she enters The Crown, the smell of bacon wafts up her nose and she instinctively orders a full English. Bacon and chocolate are her two vices… should she combine them and order a hot chocolate to wash down her meal? She decides against it, and sticks to the more traditional choice of orange juice. The pub is reasonably quiet at this time, so she can savour her breakfast before waiting for trade to pick up and start talking to the regulars.

She dives into the food, eating everything apart from the mushrooms which she has been strangely wary of since taking on the case. As she chews, she notices a flyer on the table: the pub is running a competition in which ten people who answer the puzzle correctly will win a free slap-up meal. Can you find the answer word by choosing letters from the sequence of shapes shown to spell a common seven-letter word? For instance, as the first shape shown is a square, your first letter must be R, I, T, S or Y. Each shape/letter pairing can only be used once.

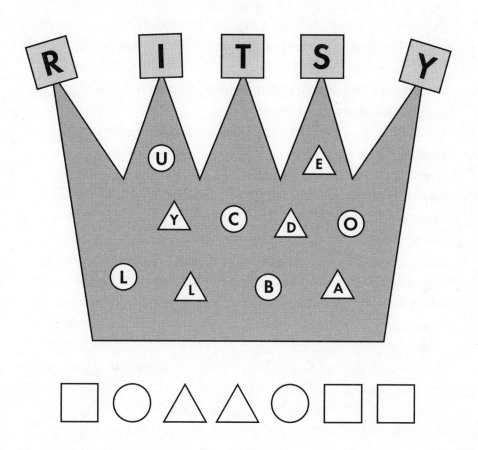

# PUB FENG SHUI

After finishing her delicious breakfast and solving the competition puzzle, Heather is less impressed when she sees the bill. She double checks it's correct with the barman who just shrugs and says "Blame inflation, not me!" before plaintively adding "I suppose I won't be getting a tip today then?"

Looking around, Heather can see that the pub has filled up slightly, and there are people sitting at ten different tables. The tables are of different sizes, and are arranged in a slightly unusual manner.

Solve this puzzle to determine the positions of each of the ten tables in the pub that people are sitting at. Four of the tables occupy a single square, three occupy two squares, two occupy three squares and one occupies four squares. Tables that occupy more than one square are positioned either horizontally or vertically. To ensure the pubgoers can easily access their table of choice, no two tables touch at any point, not even diagonally.

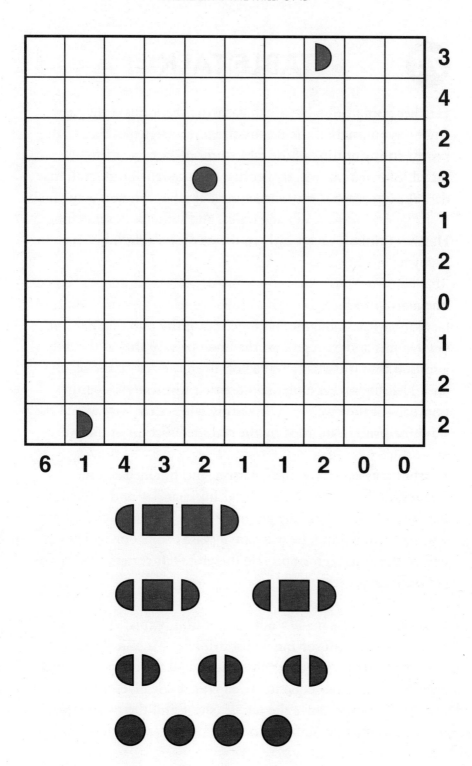

# TABLE TALK

Heather goes from table to table, asking the locals if they saw anything unusual on the day in question. After speaking to the people sitting at nine of the tables no-one has provided any useful information, mostly because they weren't in the pub that day. She approaches the tenth and final table, where a gentleman is sitting on his own, nursing a pint and some pork scratchings. Heather thinks it's a bit early in the day for alcohol, but each to his own.

The man introduces himself as Kevin, and he says that whilst he didn't witness an argument, he was in the pub that day and saw Dennis and Sam go into the more private area of the pub, a section that is partially walled off from the rest of the seating area. Heather makes a mental note that this sounds slightly unusual – if they were merely tasting wines then why would they want the privacy afforded by the secluded section of the pub?

Heather asks about the third person, and finally has some luck. Kevin says that as he finished his drink that day and walked into the car park, he saw a lady getting into a car. Although he only saw her from behind, he was sure it wasn't someone he knew, which was unusual for him. He therefore felt certain this was the person Heather was after.

Kevin says that he made a note of her numberplate on a cube puzzle he had been solving whilst drinking his pint that day. Unfortunately he solved it in pencil and all the digits and letters he entered have subsequently been erased. He gives it to Heather and says if she can solve the puzzle, she'll find the numberplate revealed in the grey squares, in order from least to most stars.

Place the numbers from 1-4 and the letters E, F, G and H once in every row and column of eight squares, which are spread over two faces of the cube, as indicated in the example. In addition, you should place 1-4 and E, F, G and H once in each of the bold-lined 2x4 rectangles.

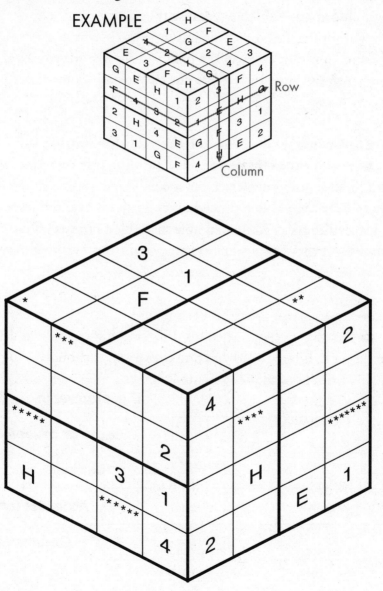

EXAMPLE

# 75 PLATE RECOGNITION

Heather thanks Kevin and asks him to wait for her inside the pub. She steps outside and calls in the numberplate to find out who it belongs to. Is she finally getting closer to determining who killed Dennis and Sam, and why?

A minute later, she receives the name of the person registered as the owner of the car. She lets out a little gasp as she hears the person's name.

Solve this puzzle to find out who the car belongs to. To do so, you must solve the crossword-style clue alongside each row of the grid, and write one letter per square. As you move down the pyramid the answer to each clue is an anagram of the answer on the row above, with one extra letter added per row. Once complete, the letters in squares numbered from 1-10 will reveal the name.

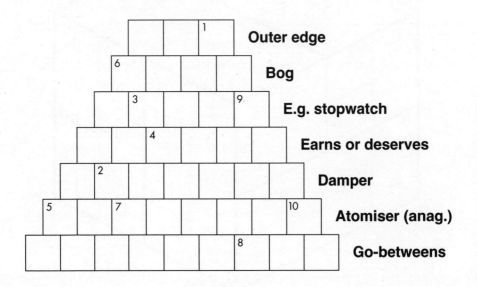

Outer edge

Bog

E.g. stopwatch

Earns or deserves

Damper

Atomiser (anag.)

Go-betweens

# 76 LAW OF AVERAGES

Heather is excited because she is now pretty sure who the Moira that Sam was referring to in his 'no good can come of this' note is. It wasn't Moira Ali after all – it was Moira Moore!

She pops her head around the pub door, and asks Kevin to join her outside. She asks if he has heard of Moira, but he shakes his head – the name Moira Moore means nothing to him.

Heather realises that whilst Moira is the registered owner of the car, it doesn't necessarily mean that it was her driving that day. There's still a chance it's pure coincidence that she is called Moira. She resolves to go and see her as soon as possible, but she wants to be sure it really was Moira driving the car and not someone else.

She asks Kevin to think hard – although he only saw her from behind, did he notice anything about her that Heather could use to help identify her as the driver of the car, perhaps a distinctive tattoo on the back of her neck or something along those lines. Kevin thinks for a moment, and then says he was pretty sure she had brown hair, although that doesn't really narrow it down much. He then suddenly says "I do know exactly how tall she is!"

Heather enquires how, and Kevin explains that his party trick is being able to look at a person and tell their height with 100% accuracy. Heather makes a wry mental note she never wants to attend a party that Kevin's at. He goes on to state that the average height of Dennis, Sam and Moira is 167 centimetres, and that the largest difference in height between the three of them is 15 centimetres. Heather knows from her notes on the deceased that Dennis was 173cm tall. Given this, how tall are Sam and Moira? Kevin sees her scratching her head and says, "As a little clue, Moira is shorter than Sam."

# RINGING A BELL

Heather drives over to see Sandy, and asks her if Sam ever mentioned someone called Moira Moore. Sandy thinks for a moment, and then says the name doesn't ring a bell. If it's someone that Sam knew, then she was presumably a name from a long time ago, before Sam and Sandy met.

Sandy enquires as to whether this is the Moira that Sam was referring to in his note, and Heather says that's her working hypothesis, but she doesn't know for sure yet.

Heather heads to the police station so that she can run a background check on Moira. As she reaches the front door of the station and reaches inside her pocket for her entry pass, she has a sinking feeling as she realises that in her eagerness to get out of the door that morning she forgot to take her ID with her.

She tries to get the attention of the duty sergeant on the front desk by waving manically, but she is disappointed when he looks up and she realises they don't know each other – he must be new to the job. Heather realises that to gain entry she will need to use the back-up system of pressing the intercom buzzer and saying the password for that week. Unfortunately she can't remember it, but has written a subtle memory reminder down on a piece of paper. Can you use this to deduce the password?

You must mentally slide each column of letters up or down, in order to reveal a common nine-letter word in the central row. There is only one possible word that can be made. What is it?

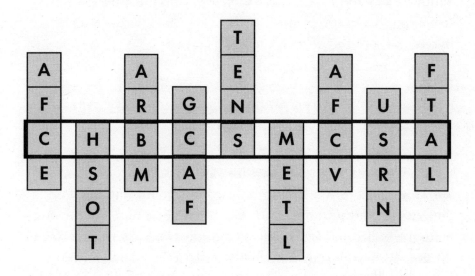

# 78 LACK OF CONVICTION

Heather finally gains access to the police station after correctly stating the password. As she reaches her desk, she is surprised to see Danni Alvarez sitting there laughing heartily and eating popcorn. She'd been watching the entry cameras and could have gone to the front desk and buzzed Heather in at any point, but apparently she found it more entertaining to watch her dancing around like a headless chicken trying to gain the duty sergeant's attention.

"Thanks, Danni – I'll remember that!"

"No problem, Hev – I'll try and dance more gracefully if I ever forget my entry card though!" Danni replies.

Heather gets to business, and runs various background checks on Moira Moore. She is disappointed to find no smoking gun, in fact she finds nothing at all: Moira has never had any run-ins with the police and is apparently squeaky clean. She writes down Moira's address. She lives in a village that is less than an hour away from Upper Gorsetown.

Heather heads straight out to go and speak to Moira. The equations show the distances to three villages in the area, in miles. All the distances are whole numbers. Given that the village Heather needs to visit is an odd number of miles away, which village is Heather travelling to?

= BRAMBLEWOOD

= BRIARWOOD

= BRACKENWOOD

$$(2 \times \text{🫐}) + \text{🍃} = 20 \text{ miles}$$

$$\text{🫐} + (2 \times \text{🌿}) = 15 \text{ miles}$$

$$(2 \times \text{🌿}) + (2 \times \text{🍃}) = 20 \text{ miles}$$

#  IN THE WEEDS

Heather heads off to Bramblewood in order to talk to Moira Moore. It is a sunny day, and with the window down she enjoys all the sounds of the countryside – the smells, not so much.

She finds Moira's home, which is a large, single-storey building that has a long driveway. She parks outside and walks up the drive so as not to make a noise; she doesn't want Moira to be forewarned of her arrival. Most of the garden is hopelessly overgrown, and clearly Moira pays little attention to it.

As she nears the house, Heather is confronted by a large pine tree with many mushrooms growing underneath it. It looks to Heather as though some of the mushrooms have been picked, which implies that Moira, or at least someone she lives with, knows a thing or two about mushrooms.

There are 14 unpicked mushrooms remaining. Can you locate them all in the grid? Four have been placed to get you started. Numbers around the edge of the grid indicate the number of mushrooms to be found in each row and column of the grid. Mushrooms cannot touch, not even diagonally.

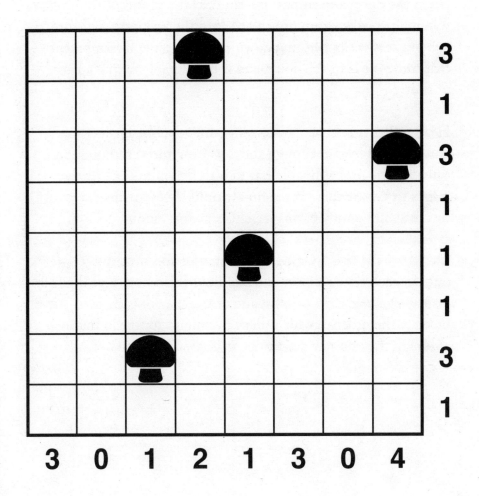

# 80     TAKE FIVE

Heather knocks on the door, but nobody answers. She puts her ear to the door, and thinks she can hear the sound of running water. She walks around to the back of the property, and sure enough sees water running down the drainpipe. It is apparent that someone is in the house and is presumably taking a bath or shower.

Heather has no choice but to wait patiently. She is eager for answers, and feels as though she is waiting forever, though in actuality she probably only has to wait five minutes. Heather muses to herself that, in the highly unlikely event they ever turn this case into a movie, this scene is ripe for culling.

Can you 'take five' by solving this puzzle? You must place 1-9 once in each row, column and 3x3 bold-lined box. Five digits are displayed above each column and at the start of each row. These indicate the order in which those five digits appear in that region, although they do not need to be in consecutive squares.

| | 15849 | 15738 | 49872 | 49825 | 85361 | 37968 | 82165 | 74352 | 56429 |
|---|---|---|---|---|---|---|---|---|---|
| 14938 | | | | | | | | | |
| 78126 | | | | | | | | | |
| 75913 | | | | | | | | | |
| 16578 | | | | | | | | | |
| 57632 | | | | | | | | | |
| 83279 | | | | | | | | | |
| 37968 | | | | | | | | | |
| 81562 | | | | | | | | | |
| 65384 | | | | | | | | | |

# 81 SHOW ME THE MONEY

Heather knocks again, and this time the door is answered by a red-faced lady with brown hair who is fairly short. Heather believes it to be Moira – she doesn't have Kevin's gift of being able to tell height perfectly, but she seems to be around the height he said.

"Moira Moore? My name is Detective Heather Vintner."

The lady looks surprised and nods, before adding "Sorry if you've been knocking for a while – I've been in the shower. I've been weeding all morning and got rather sweaty."

Heather is surprised given the state of the front garden, but in fairness when she walked around the back she saw a wheelbarrow and a couple of nice flowerbeds that looked like they'd been planted very recently, judging by the loose earth. "I've always had green fingers," continues Moira, "or green thumb as my son would say. Awful, isn't it? He's at university now, but thanks to the internet he's grown up speaking American English, not 'proper' English. He calls candyfloss 'cotton candy' and all sorts. Can you imagine?" She then pauses abruptly before adding "Sorry, I always jabber on when I'm nervous. How can I help you?" Heather is not here for small talk, so dives right in and tells Moira that she has reason to believe she was one of the last people to see Dennis and Sam alive.

Moira quickly acknowledges that she knew both men. She explains:

"I was actually at university with Sam and Dennis. The three of us were good friends. This sounds like a tall story, but early one morning in our second year we were walking back to our hall of residence feeling a little worse for wear after a night on the tiles, when Dennis stumbled and fell over by some hedges. From that unusual angle he espied the strap of a large holdall behind a tree in one of the lanes. We dragged it out, opened it up, and imagine our surprise when we found it was full of cash! Presumably a thief had burgled a shop and then got spooked and done a runner for some reason, dumping the cash in a hurry perhaps to come back for later. Well, I'm just guessing, we have no idea how it got there really.

"We had two clear options: hand it in to the police, or keep it for ourselves. Well, as impoverished students, we decided in a split second to keep the money, and when you commit to something like that you can't really change your mind a few days later, can you? It's a bit like a lie that runs out of control and ends up taking on a life of its own."

"What happened next?" Heather says, trying to temper her incredulity.

"We decided we'd bury it for a long period of time so that, if anyone was searching for the money, the trail would run cold and no-one would be looking for the serial numbers on the bank notes anymore. Then we'd split the money, a third each, and spend it however we wished. We counted and there was about £30,000 pounds in there! Sam and Dennis took it and buried it in a wood in Upper Gorsetown, where they were both born. Only the three of us knew the exact location, of course."

"And how many years did you decide to bury it for?" asks Heather.

Solve the following puzzle and sum up the digits in the squares containing asterisks to find out the answer. Fill the white squares so that the sum total of each across or down run of squares matches the total at the start of that run. A number cannot repeat within a run, and you must use numbers from 1-9 only.

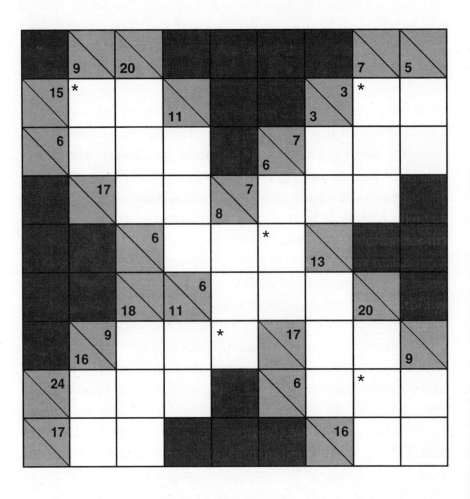

# HARD TIMES

Heather nods in acknowledgement, furiously writing down everything Moira tells her in her unique shorthand. Moira continues:

"Anyhow, things have been a bit tricky for me of late – I have had some…. difficulties… and have been struggling to make ends meet. That money would come in really handy, and it's almost twenty years anyhow, so a couple of weeks ago I decided to contact Sam and Dennis. Well, all I had was a phone number for Dennis, who had promised he would never, ever change his mobile number so we could always get in touch with each other, and I'd likewise always kept the same number. However, when I rang his number I got that annoying 'number not recognised' message, so he clearly didn't stick to his word.

"I thought that maybe it was just an honest mistake so, remembering where the money was buried, I went there with the intention of taking £10,000 out and leaving a note for the other two to let them know I'd taken my share."

"And what did you find when you located and dug up the bag?" Heather asks, intrigued by this tale that is so strange it is probably true.

Moira is extremely agitated after being asked this question, and answers in a strange code. Can you work out what she says?

ELUFEMA LX ROQNQERA VGAM E DIOMC KIIRA AUQSG, COF ES ON, UMC DIOMC SGUS SGAQA VUR MISGEMF SGAQA ZOS SGA ALNSX ZUF! MIS IMKX GUC SGAX BKAUQKX SUJAM SGA LIMAX DIQ SGALRAKTAR, E'C VUFAQ SGAX CEC ES DUEQKX QABAMSKX SII.

# LADY LUCK

"I was furious, of course," continues Moira, although she has calmed down by now and started talking normally again. "I kept opening and closing the bag, hoping to see the money magically appear. It makes no sense, of course, but I suppose I acted a bit like how you do when you're waiting at a pedestrian crossing for ages and you start pressing the button a few more times to try to speed things up, even though you know deep down it makes no difference." Heather chuckles to herself quietly – she'd definitely been known to do that herself.

Moira continues: "I had no way of knowing where Sam or Dennis were: they could have moved away from Upper Gorsetown years ago. I know it's a fairly small place but if there are a thousand people living there I could hardly go knocking door-to-door on the off-chance Dennis or Sam opens the door, could I?"

Heather nods – if you stuck around the area keeping a low profile for a few days then you might bump into one of them but it certainly wasn't a trivial matter to find them. Given this, Heather asks what she decided to do next.

"Nothing! That's the God's honest truth. But, by sheer coincidence, I'd arranged to meet up with my half-brother who I hadn't seen for months that weekend, and he came round for a roast. His name's Gus Hawkins, he owns The Crown pub in Upper Gorsetown. We're close but rarely see each other in person; families can be like that, you know? I suppose you might have come across him at some point. I'd never told him, or anyone else, about the money. Well anyway, he started talking about mushrooms – I like to forage for them, you see – and he mentioned in passing someone called 'Dennis'. I asked if it was Dennis Baker, and he confirmed it was. Serendipity, I suppose you'd call it! Anyway, I was that annoyed that I told him everything, all about the money and the deal I had made with Sam and Dennis. It felt good to share the secret with someone after all these years, to be honest. He was very calm about it. When I told him I had debts I was struggling to pay, he said he'd do all he could to help me out."

Heather asks Moira why she didn't just contact her half-brother as soon as she couldn't reach Dennis or Sam by phone. She replies that at the time she had no intention of ever sharing the secret with anyone, and she could hardly enquire about Dennis or Sam without explaining why she wanted to contact them.

Heather then asks why Moira needs the money so badly. Solve this puzzle to find out the cause of her debts. You must create words by moving from the letter inside a diamond to a connected diamond. All words you make must include the letter in the large diamond at the centre of the diagram, and you may use the letter in a diamond more than once in a word. How many words can you find? Try to find at least 10 words. The longest word that can be made in the diagram is the cause of Moira's debts.

# 84 YOUR NUMBER'S UP

Moira says that Gus had given her Dennis's phone number. He'd had it ever since Dennis won a competition in the pub and he'd phoned to tell him the good news.

"Anyway, I called the number straight away – no point wasting time, is there? Funnily enough he was with Sam at the time so I spoke to them both on speakerphone. They seemed very surprised to hear from me, and very evasive. I asked to meet up with them to discuss the money – of course, I didn't tell them I already knew it wasn't there. Well, after a bit of dithering and pretending they had a bad line, they hung up on me, the cheek of it! I could swear Sam was deliberately stuttering to feign interference on the line!"

"And Gus listened to the call?" Heather clarifies.

"Yes, yes, he was listening in. He didn't speak, of course."

"And what number did you call Dennis on? So I can check it matches the number I have on file."

Find the phone number that Moira called by solving this puzzle. To do so, place the numbers 1-9 once in each row, column and 3x3 bold-lined box. In addition, you must also place 1-9 once each in the letters of the word C, A, L, L. These extra regions are indicated in grey in the grid. Once you have solved the puzzle, enter the numbers in squares that contain asterisks reading left-to-right, top-to-bottom in the placeholders below the grid.

|   |   |   |   |   |   |   |   |   |
|---|---|---|---|---|---|---|---|---|
| 2 |   |   |   |   |   |   |   | * |
|   |   |   | *7 |   | 9 |   |   |   |
| * |   |   | 1 |   |   |   |   |   |
|   |   | 9 | *3 |   |   | 1 | * | 6 |
|   | *4 | 6 |   |   |   | 3 | 9 | * |
| 8 | * | 1 | * |   | 2 | 4 |   |   |
|   | * |   |   |   | 5 |   |   |   |
|   |   |   | 9 |   | 4 |   | * |   |
|   |   |   |   |   |   |   |   | 9 |

**PHONE NUMBER: _ _ _ _ _   _ _ _ _ _ _**

# 85 WHAT HAPPENED NEXT?

Heather enquires as to what Moira did after the call: did she resolve to go and have it out with Dennis and Sam, given Gus probably also knew where they both lived?

Moira shakes her head and says that, whilst deeply annoyed, she wanted to give it some thought and not act hastily. She could hardly go to the police, given she might get in trouble over hiding all that money years ago! She also mentions that Gus told her to bide her time: he thought it likely they were spooked by the call and would contact her a few days later when they had reconsidered things and offer to meet up.

Heather doesn't comment on whether Moira will get arrested for her role in hiding stolen money, though she will certainly check on it when back at base. Moira then adds:

"Funnily enough, a few days later I had a call from Sam. But not the one I expected. Instead of offering to meet up to discuss things like adults, he told me in no uncertain terms to leave him alone and not to think about threatening him. Well, that made no sense to me. I assume he was just trying to stop me pursuing things further but still, it was an odd move.

Anyhow, I felt like I was going round in circles. I'd tried to contact them, with no joy, then tried to dig up the money, but it wasn't there. I'd then got their phone number, but they refused to see me, and then I'd had that strange call warning me off from Sam."

Solve this puzzle to find out how Moira felt. You must choose one letter from each ring to make a word, working inwards from the outer ring to the inner ring. There is only one possible word that can be made.

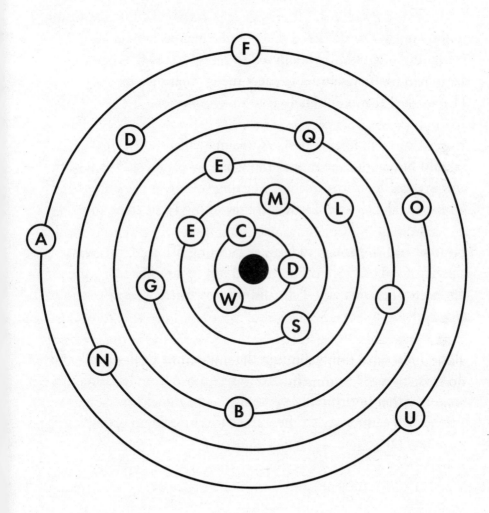

#  SURPRISE, SURPRISE

Moira is clearly in a talkative mood, and continues: "Anyhow, a week later Gus called me to see if there were any updates. I mentioned the call from Sam and that they basically wanted nothing to do with me. He was disappointed, of course, wanting to look out for me. What a nice man! Anyhow, he had an intriguing suggestion. He offered to set up a surprise meeting with them as they refused to meet me of their own free will. He was sure that would help lead to a resolution.

Neither of them knew that Gus was my half-brother, or that I'd told him about the money. So when he contacted them both and invited them to a free wine tasting session at the pub, they jumped at the chance. Little did they know I'd be there too!"

Heather had to hand it to Gus: as cunning plans go, this was a pretty good one. She'd find it hard not to attend a free wine tasting too, particularly if she didn't know there were any strings attached.

To find out what Gus promised them, discover the longest word that can be made in the grid. You must move from letter to letter, moving either horizontally, vertically or diagonally one square at a time. You cannot revisit the same letter more than once.

| | | | |
|---|---|---|---|
| E | W | V | M |
| R | N | A | P |
| T | H | G | A |
| C | L | O | S |

#  DIGGING UP THE PAST

Moira explains that when she arrived at the pub her half-brother had ensured that Dennis and Sam were already fairly merry, hoping that this might loosen their lips and make them more amenable. "I went into the private area, where they were sipping wine, and they both looked like they'd seen a ghost! I was the last person they'd expected to see. I asked for my fair share of the money, explaining that I'd fallen on hard times. Initially they said they couldn't remember where it was – Dennis gave me some baloney about having the co-ordinates engraved on his wedding ring which he'd lost, and Sam muttered something about he couldn't remember where the money was either.

I told them that was funny, as I could remember where it was, I'd been there to take a look and knew it had already gone! Well, they looked at each other, stuttered a bit and then finally admitted that they did remember where it was, after all. Dennis said he checked on it annually, and the last time he did so the money had gone. Vanished into thin air, he said. More like vanished into his back pocket, I'm sure! They swore blind that they had no idea who took it, and started blaming people with metal detectors going around searching for treasure, or some nonsense like that. Last time I checked there's no metal in banknotes – did they think about that when concocting the sorry story?

Then Dennis pulled out his phone and started trying to show me a photo of the empty bag in the hole, as if that proved anything. Clearly, he'd emptied the bag of the money, and then taken the photo. They must think I was born yesterday! I started shouting as much, but they insisted they were telling the truth, and then I stormed out of the place!"

Take a look at these six empty bags. Only one of them matches the larger bag exactly: can you spot which one?

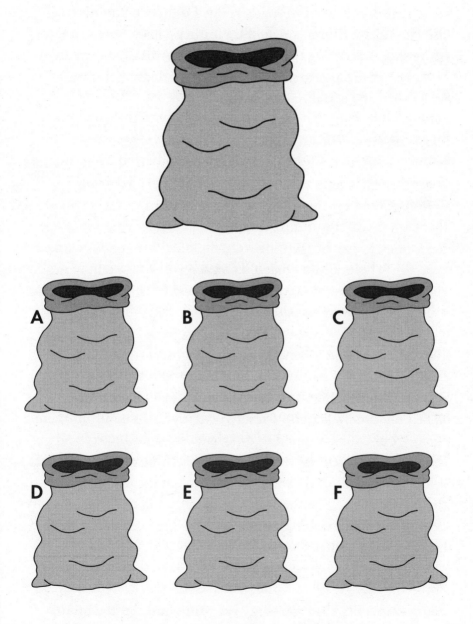

# 88 REVENGE IS A DISH BEST SERVED COLD

"And that brings us up-to-date, really. I didn't do anything else after that," Moira concludes. Heather pauses for a second, processing everything that Moira has said. At least she finally knows what the argument in the pub was about, and it was odder than she could have ever expected.

"So… let me get this straight," says Heather incredulously. "You believe these men helped themselves to £10,000 of 'your' money, are clearly extremely annoyed about it, but decided to do… nothing? They say that three people can keep a secret if two of them are dead – I put it to you that it was really you who took the money to pay off your debts, then killed Sam and Dennis to keep this whole sordid affair a secret forever. You're telling me an alternative version of events that is a blend of fact and fiction in order to cover your tracks."

"No, no, everything I've told you is the gospel truth," Moira insists. "Besides, I hadn't done anything about their duplicity, it's true. But that doesn't mean I planned to let it lie forever. When the time was right, I resolved to myself to confront them again – I of course wanted to do whatever I could to try and get them to at least tell the truth. I wasn't planning anything illegal, mind. And to think – I was probably one of the last people to see them both alive." She then adds wistfully, "And my chances of getting my hands on the money are gone forever now those two have got their comeuppance!"

"Indeed," says Heather, "quite the coincidence, don't you think? You seem sadder that you won't get your hands on the money than you are about the deaths of these two men, if I might say so. And what of your half-brother?"

"As I said, I stormed out, so I didn't have time to talk to him there and then. He messaged me afterwards to ask how it went, and I sent him an email to explain what had happened – take a look. If I'm making this all up, why would I have done that?"

The email that Moira shows Heather is encoded, can you work out what it says?

GURL SVANYYL NQZVGGRQ GUNG GURL UNQ QHT HC GUR ONT OHG VAFVFGRQ GUNG JURA GURL QVQ FB VG JNF RZCGL. V QBA'G ORYVRIR N JBEQ GUNG GURL FNL, BS PBHEFR. PYRNEYL GURL'IR URYCRQ GURZFRYIRF GB GUR ZBARL. V PNA'G TB GB GUR CBYVPR OHG V PNA'G YRG GUVF ERFG. V'YY UNIR N GUVAX NOBHG VG SBE N JUVYR NAQ JBEX BHG UBJ GB CEBPRRQ.

# 89 CAUGHT ON CAMERA

Heather informs Moira that, given the seriousness of the matter at hand, she is going to have to provide an alibi as to her whereabouts on the evening and night in question.

Moira says that she was at home all night – and she can prove it. She had lots of cameras installed all around the property a couple of years ago after a break-in. She takes Heather to her computer and shows her the relevant footage from the cameras in the bungalow. It certainly appears as though Moira's alibi is watertight: moving from camera to camera, Heather can track her movements from room to room, before retiring to bed for the night and then getting up the following morning after the body of Dennis was discovered.

Heather just wants to be sure there are no blind spots, so walks around carefully noting down the locations of all the cameras. In the grid, there are two cameras positioned in each row, column and bold-outlined region. Cameras never touch horizontally, vertically or diagonally. Use logic to determine where all the cameras are positioned.

**RING BEARER**

Satisfied that Moira was indeed at home, and that there are no significant blind spots in the camera coverage, Heather is convinced she either isn't the murderer, or at least didn't act alone.

As Heather drives away from the bungalow, she realises that Gus is clearly more involved than she had ever realised and she needs to talk to him. But now she knows there is money involved, she needs to talk to Sandy and Gemma, too. She visits them both right away.

Sandy is surprised to hear about the money, and says that Sam had never mentioned it to her. She asks if this could be related to the £10,000 transfer he had received from Dennis. Heather says it could be, but doesn't know for sure. Although she keeps it to herself, the idea that they dug up the money doesn't really make sense to Heather: why would they do so after almost 20 years of leaving it alone, and at the exact time that Moira also wanted it, but before she was able to contact them to alert them that she did? Were they psychic? And even if they had done so, why not split the money equally so that they each received £15,000? Something wasn't right with that version of events.

Her conversation with Gemma is more interesting. Gemma instantly seems quite defensive when Heather mentions the money but, like Sandy, she says she doesn't know anything about it. Heather is certain she is bluffing. Gemma starts fiddling with the ring on her finger, but being a bit loose it falls on the floor. Gemma lurches forward to pick it up, but Heather beats her to it and as she picks it up she notices it really is engraved, and bears the wording OAK 9,3.

Heather says nothing, but reading '9.3' triggers something in her memory, and she recalls that at Sam's house she found a strange message that read 'LOCATION IS ROW NINE COLUMN THREE'. Heather now sees that this must have been referring to the location where the bag of money had been buried! It was the exact location where some of Jeremy's blood had been found, and there was loose earth.

Her heart starts beating faster as an idea occurs to her – Gemma found out about the money, and is in cahoots with Jeremy. They dug it up in order to share it – possibly to start a new life together. They've killed Dennis and Sam so they could never find out it was gone and cause trouble, and then invented a pretend argument between themselves to cover their tracks! They wouldn't have known about Moira, or if they did maybe she was next on their hit list.

Heather comes inside the house and says she needs to have a look around. Gemma asks why, and Heather says she has reason to believe that Gemma may have been involved in the murders of the two men. She gasps and suddenly gets very upset.

Heather isn't certain Gemma is the murderer, but at the very least believes she is hiding something. If she had to put a figure on it, she would say the probability that Gemma is telling the truth about everything is the same as picking three cards at random from a standard deck of 52 cards and them all being red. What is Heather's figure?

# 91 A SPOT OF BOTHER

As Heather looks around the house, she tries to work things out in her head: it stacks up that Gemma and Jeremy are the guilty parties, and it's true that they at least partly provided each other's alibis. Money does strange things to people, she muses.

Heather doesn't find anything of note until she comes to the kitchen. She sees a pile of jumpers next to the partially-filled washing machine. It appears that Gemma was about to put a wash on when Heather rang the bell. She looks through all the jumpers, and espies a little spot of blood on one of them. When challenged, Gemma says she has no idea where it came from. She'd worn that particular jumper on the day of the memorial service and, as far as she could remember, hadn't accidentally cut herself that day. She must have done though, and it was without doubt her blood.

Heather puts the jumper in a plastic bag, and informs Gemma she'll send it away for priority testing. Gemma protests loudly – and perhaps desperately – that if she had anything to hide, she'd have washed it straight away. Nevertheless, Heather isn't taking any chances. She decides not to arrest Gemma there and then: she still needs to talk to Gus. She leaves, drops off the evidence for testing back at the station, then goes home for the evening and some well-deserved rest.

The jumper that had the spot of blood on it was at the bottom of the pile – can you work out which one it is?

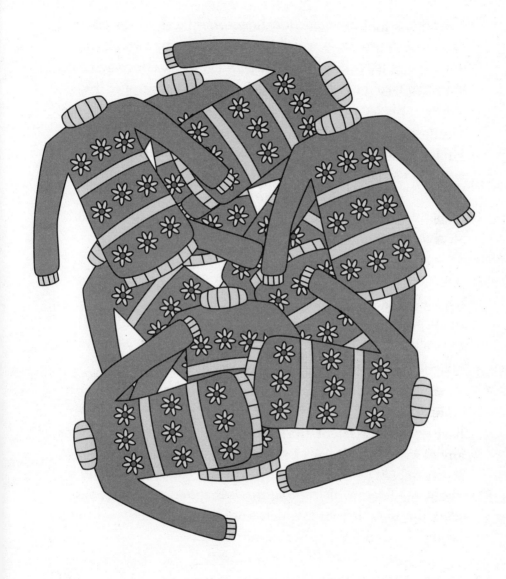

# 92 PUB LUNCH

The next day, Heather spends the morning reviewing everything she has learnt so far. With all the details buzzing around her head, she goes to The Crown pub to talk to Gus. He's a bit flustered, trying to get the swanky new voice-controlled TV screen in the bar to work. Heather hears him say "Turn up the volume" and then a second later a disembodied voice from the TV responds with the words "Sorry, I don't understand what you mean by turnip the volume, please try again." Gus mutters to himself, "Useless thing, I thought this tech was supposed to work properly nowadays." He suddenly becomes aware of Heather's presence in his peripheral vision, and looks up.

"Here for lunch?" he enquires, as he sees her approach the bar. Heather shakes her head – she wishes she was as she's feeling rather peckish – but she has serious business to attend to. They go to a private area of the pub so that they can talk without anyone overhearing them. Gus's expression turns serious.

Heather tells Gus as much as she is prepared for him to know at this stage. She asks why he lied about not knowing who the person arguing with Sam and Dennis was, given it was his own half-sister! He looks visibly shocked that Heather has found out who it was, from which she surmises that perhaps Moira hasn't filled him in on her visit, which would count in her favour, if so. Though he could just be acting surprised.

Gus says that it was a very delicate situation, and he has always been protective of his half-sister. Knowing that it was a murder enquiry and that his sister could be implicated, he had simply wanted to keep her away from it all. She gets stressed easily, he says, and couldn't cope with a police investigation. It was a harmless little white lie as he was sure she was innocent, and that was the only reason he'd been liberal with the truth.

He asks how she found out, and when Heather mentions Kevin he says some disparaging things about him, particularly given he is presumably one of his best customers! How does Gus sum up Kevin? Solve this puzzle to find out. You must find the word that will fill the empty boxes on each line in order to link the first word with the second word to create two new compound words or phrases. For instance, the word 'chip' could link the words 'blue' and 'shop' to create 'blue chip' and 'chip shop'. Once complete, the grey squares will reveal the answer.

SOAP ☐☐☐ OFFICE

NIGHT ☐☐☐☐ SANDWICH

SLIDE ☐☐☐☐ BUSINESS

PRIVATE ☐☐☐ WITNESS

PIGGY ☐☐☐☐ HOLIDAY

CASH ☐☐☐ CHART

CRASH ☐☐☐☐ LINE

SKELETON ☐☐☐ SIGNATURE

# MONEY TALKS

Heather asks Gus about the money, and how he had felt when Moira told him about the large sum of money that she, Dennis and Sam had found all those years ago, and their agreement to split it? More to the point, when Moira said she suspected they had taken it but then discovered they didn't want to talk to her about it, what was his reaction?

Gus admits to being taken aback by the whole affair, but tells her that he had promised to support Moira as much as he could, in a peaceful and amicable way, which is why he had suggested the clandestine meeting and hopefully a calm chat, rather than going in all guns blazing.

Heather then asks what his reaction had been when he'd received Moira's email informing him that the strategy hadn't worked, and that she was now certain they had helped themselves to the money and cut her out of the agreement. Gus tells her that it was of course very annoying, but that Moira had wanted to bide her time to work out what to do next, if anything, and he fully supported that decision. Heather decides to apply some further pressure:

"So, despite being so protective of Moira, and believing she was clearly wronged, you were very happy and content to just wait and do nothing? You didn't decide to take matters into your own hands and, accidentally or intentionally, exact the ultimate revenge?"

Gus splutters that he categorically wouldn't do such a thing, protesting that it is out of the question and would go completely against his most fundamental beliefs. Besides, by the time he'd got Moira's message saying she'd made no progress, Dennis and Sam had already left the pub.

Heather suspects that Gus's description of himself may be a red herring to throw her off the scent. Solve this puzzle to work out how he described himself. You must create an eight-letter word using the seven letters in bold below, together with just one of the letters in grey, three of which are red herrings:

# PICSFIT MEAN

#  PRESSURE COOKER

Heather says that if that's a true description of his character, he has nothing to hide and therefore nothing to worry about. Gus nods grimly, but certainly looks worried. Heather picks up on this and steps up the pressure even more by demanding to search the kitchens there and then. Gus agrees to let her take a look around.

Heather knows that Dennis and Sam most likely ate poisonous mushrooms in the early evening. If Gus had somehow met up with them again after Moira had left, and poisoned them, then he'd have likely prepared the mushrooms in the kitchen. Clearly the food waste would be long gone, but it was very easy to slip up and inadvertently not dispose of potential evidence.

Heather looks through the bins – a smelly and unpleasant task – but doesn't find anything untoward. She sees bits of mushroom stalk, but she is sure they are from some empty packets of large portobello mushrooms served by the pub as part of its popular full English breakfasts.

The floor looks very clean. Nothing if not thorough, Heather gets down on her hands and knees and crawls along the floor, looking under each of the units with a torch to illuminate the shadows. As anyone obsessed with hoovering knows to their chagrin, nooks and crannies are almost impossible to keep completely clean. Sure enough, under one of the giant fridges in the food preparation area, Heather espies some bits of food detritus, which she sweeps out with her baton. She can't be sure, but she thinks one of them might be a fragment of dried mushroom. She bags up the evidence for testing at the lab.

Heather can identify what some of the bits of food waste are that have been mixed together. Can you do the same by solving this puzzle successfully? Three vegetables have had their letters all scrambled together here. What are they? None of them are plurals.

# SCOOPING

# PIRANHA

# SAUNAS

# SAFE HAVEN

Heather asks to see Gus's private office which is located in a room above the pub. Reluctantly, he allows her to search it. The room is a mess of papers and bills. He is clearly better at running the front of house operation than dealing with the financial side of running a business. As she rummages around, she finds nothing of note.

Just as she is about to leave, Heather spots a safe positioned behind a desk, and asks Gus for the code. He says he hasn't opened the safe for a long time so can't remember it, but Heather can see some fingerprints on the front of the safe surrounded by dust, suggesting it has been opened recently. Gus is surprised to see this and says it certainly wasn't him. He says that whilst he can't remember the code off the top of his head, he carries a reminder with him in the form of a puzzle that reveals it when solved.

He pulls out his wallet, and gives Heather the following note. Can you use it to work out the four-digit code and open the safe?

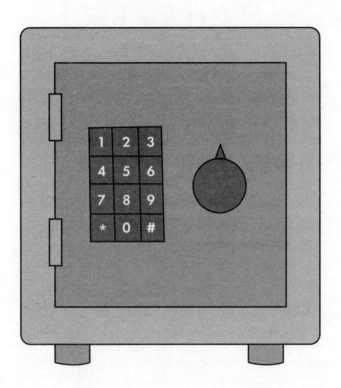

My first and third digits sum to 8

My second and fourth digits sum to 13

I contain only one of the numbers 1,3,5,7,9

My first digit is greater than my last

My second digit is less than my last

# HIGH STAKES

The safe swings open. Heather puts gloves on, and rummages around inside. She feels a hard object hidden underneath a false lining at the bottom of the safe. She pulls out a steak knife, which looks clean to the eye but she wagers might well contain tiny traces of Dennis's blood. Gus protests his innocence, and says he's never seen the knife before. If he'd hidden it there, why on earth would he have voluntarily given Heather the hint to the safe code? It would make no sense.

Heather realises she is facing the same dilemma she'd had recently with Gemma: to make an arrest there and then, or wait on the results of the tests. As she can't actually see blood on the knife, she decides not to arrest Gus but to wait to see what the tests on the knife and food debris show. She leaves, and takes the evidence she has gathered straight for testing.

The following day, after a sleepless night, the results of the tests are in. The knife did indeed contain minuscule amounts of blood – just enough to be able to make a match.

Can you work out which of the people from A to D the DNA sample from the blood on the knife matched with? The sample will appear somewhere in one of the four grids in a 3x2 rectangle, as shown at the top of the next page: do not rotate the rectangle.

## DNA sample to find:

| A | C | G |
|---|---|---|
| T | A | C |

**A**

| T | A | C | A | A | C | C | G | G | G |
|---|---|---|---|---|---|---|---|---|---|
| A | G | A | C | A | T | T | G | C | T |
| T | A | C | T | C | T | C | T | A | A |
| T | G | T | A | C | T | C | C | T | A |
| A | A | C | C | C | T | A | A | C | T |
| A | G | A | G | A | A | C | C | T | C |
| A | C | A | A | T | A | T | C | C | G |
| A | A | C | G | G | G | C | A | T | C |
| A | C | T | T | G | A | A | A | C | C |
| A | C | A | A | C | A | A | A | G | G |

**B**

| C | G | C | T | A | G | A | T | A | C |
|---|---|---|---|---|---|---|---|---|---|
| G | C | G | C | G | G | C | T | C | C |
| T | A | T | A | G | A | T | A | A | A |
| A | C | A | C | C | C | A | A | A | A |
| C | A | G | A | C | C | G | C | T | A |
| C | G | C | T | T | C | A | A | T | C |
| A | C | C | A | G | A | A | A | C | G |
| G | A | A | G | C | T | T | T | T | C |
| T | T | A | C | G | A | C | T | A |   |
| G | A | C | T | T | C | T | C | C | A |

**C**

| A | T | C | C | A | A | A | A | A | T |
|---|---|---|---|---|---|---|---|---|---|
| A | C | A | T | T | C | T | C | T | A |
| C | A | A | C | G | C | A | C | C | C |
| C | T | A | A | C | A | C | C | C | G |
| A | C | A | T | G | A | T | G | G | C |
| T | T | T | T | A | C | C | A | A | A |
| A | T | C | T | G | C | A | C | C | A |
| C | G | C | A | T | C | G | C | T | G |
| C | T | G | A | C | G | A | C | A | A |
| G | C | A | T | A | C | T | A | C | G |

**D**

| C | A | A | A | G | A | G | A | A | C |
|---|---|---|---|---|---|---|---|---|---|
| C | A | A | C | G | A | A | A | G | C |
| A | C | A | A | A | A | A | T | A | G |
| C | T | A | A | C | C | A | G | T | T |
| A | C | C | C | A | T | C | T | T | A |
| T | A | G | C | C | A | A | A | G | G |
| G | G | A | A | C | A | A | G | C | T |
| A | C | G | A | C | G | A | C | T | C |
| T | A | A | C | C | G | C | A | A | C |
| A | C | T | G | C | C | A | C | C | G |

# A SPANNER IN THE WORKS

Sample C was taken from Dennis Baker – the blood on the knife is his, as Heather had guessed it would be. Furthermore, tests on the tiny bits of food she retrieved from the kitchen floor in the pub have revealed that they contain traces of the poisonous mushroom, fool's funnel.

Heather discusses the results with her colleague Danni Alvarez.

"Can I arrest Gus right now then, do you think?"

"Not so fast, Hev," counsels Danni. "You're going to need to look at this other result first. The test performed on Gemma's jumper has come back. It shows that the blood on it belongs to none other than Dennis Baker! That throws a spanner in the works, doesn't it?" Heather scratches her head and says:

"This is so confusing! Was it Gemma? And if so, was she acting alone or in cahoots with Jeremy? Or was it Gus? And if so, was he acting alone or with his half-sister Moira egging him on? We found traces of the mushrooms in Gus's kitchen and the knife in his safe, but he gave me the code for it which is odd if he's the guilty party. Maybe he is the victim of an elaborate set-up? Gemma certainly had a good reason – if my working theory that she found and took the money is right, she would have committed the crime to ensure that she was able to keep the money and got her ex-husband out of the picture at the same time, something I'm sure Jeremy would have been happy to help with. Sam would have just been collateral damage."

Heather tries to join all the pieces of the puzzle together. Can you do likewise? You must place the nine pieces of the puzzle into the empty grid to create a valid crossword solution. Some words relate to the case. Do not rotate any of the pieces.

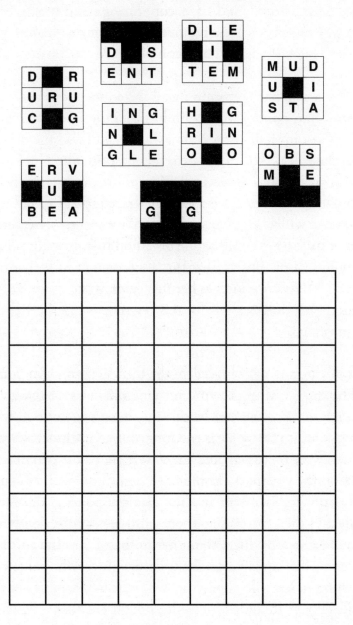

# WHODUNIT?

In time-honoured fashion, Heather wheels out a giant corkboard and pins the names and faces of her possible suspects and the victims on the board, and starts connecting them with pieces of string. She ends up with something resembling a chaotic spider's web, with bits of string all over the place.

She takes a step back, examining all the connections and timelines, and ponders. Her mind studies the faces of Gemma, Jeremy, Gus, his half-sister Moira Moore, and also the other people she has looked into. She remembers Gemma looking happy at the memorial service and standing out by her choice of jumper. She ponders the fact that Jeremy spoke about forgiveness, which jogs her memory that someone gave Father Stibley a surprising confession. Her mind turns to Gus – he's every bit as suspicious as Gemma. These two must be her main suspects. It's also not lost on her that Jeremy and Gemma have provided each other's alibis for the key time when the victims were poisoned.

She looks around at the faces on the board. There's also Judith, who she suspected until her watertight alibi arose; but was she too quick to discount her? It suddenly occurs to her that whilst she knew Judith's new partner, Connor, was at dinner when the two men were poisoned, and there were meals for two people shown on the receipt, he could have been there with anyone and simply provided her with an alibi. Heather ponders this for a minute and then moves on. There's also Sam's wife, Sandy, who seems to know very little about her husband… is she a little too innocent? Next up is Layla, Dennis's daughter, who inherited everything in his will: surely she was right to discount her from the off. Finally, there is Moira Ali, though Heather is convinced that she was a case of 'the wrong Moira' so her face is only really up on the board for completeness.

After pausing for a few minutes, she smiles to herself as if a lightbulb has gone off in her head, then furiously starts to relink various pieces of string. "Don't mess it up now, Heather," she thinks. It's her time to shine, to solve the crime and bring the perpetrator, or perpetrators, to justice. Heather thinks she finally knows who did it.

If she's correct in her deductions, it will be possible to place each unique letter of WHO DID IT? (D, H, I, O, T, W) once in each row and column of the grid below, and also once per set of six boxes joined together with string.

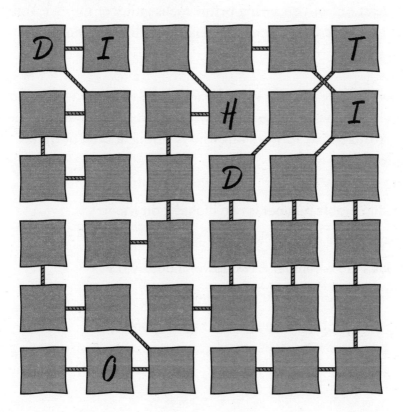

# LAST ORDERS

Heather's boss agrees with her chain of reasoning and the deductions she has made. She's finally ready to serve justice. Not without a sense of theatre, she orders six people to come to the pub, and duly sits them down at tables she has placed side by side, and which she has numbered from 1-6.

The six people she summons to the pub are Gemma, Jeremy, Moira Moore, Judith, Gus and Layla.

Heather looks at them all shifting nervously in their seats. After a long pause, Heather starts talking:

"At least one of you sitting before me is guilty of murder. You tried to cover your tracks, and you did well… but not well enough."

Upon hearing Heather's words two of the six, seated at the first and last of the six tables, start sweating profusely. Who are they? Solve this puzzle to work out who is sitting at each of the six tables.

– Judith's table number is two higher than Moira's

– Layla is not at table three, nor is Judith

– Gus's table number is two lower than Layla's

– Moira is not adjacent to Gemma

– Jeremy's table number is two higher than Layla's

# 100 MURDER WILL OUT

Heather gives them each the piece of paper below, and says:
"Write down where you're all sitting. Can you work out why
I placed you where I did?"

| 1 | | | | | |
|---|---|---|---|---|---|
| 2 | | | | | |
| 3 | | | | | |
| 4 | | | | | |
| 5 | | | | | |
| 6 | | | | | |

Layla puts her hand up – as if in school – and gives the correct
answer. Heather nods in approval.

"Well done, Layla, a nice final flourish, I think you'll all agree.
As a reward for getting the answer I can let you know right
now – you are innocent." Layla relaxes a little, but not a lot: she
already knew she didn't do it and also knows her mum is one of
the prime suspects. Given she never trusted Jeremy, she worries
that he could easily have led her astray.

As some of the six squirm uncomfortably in their chairs, Heather
gives them another piece of paper and says:

"I've had to put a lot of thought into cracking this case. Find all
these words that relate to it in the grid. They might be hidden
horizontally, vertically or diagonally and in either a forwards or
backwards direction."

She waits for everyone to solve the puzzle. She notices that Gemma and Jeremy are still sweating. Can you solve it?

| G | E | D | N | O | P | L | L | I | M | U | J |
|---|---|---|---|---|---|---|---|---|---|---|---|
| E | P | R | E | E | M | Y | J | U | R | J | U |
| D | I | O | V | T | H | G | R | S | O | S | F |
| E | N | O | I | J | U | D | H | A | O | A | O |
| H | B | V | D | S | E | H | S | A | L | A | R |
| S | W | M | E | R | O | K | N | I | A | A | A |
| E | W | I | N | M | N | N | B | S | M | L | G |
| I | S | K | C | N | I | I | I | O | S | T | I |
| L | Y | E | E | I | S | T | E | N | S | I | N |
| S | T | C | E | P | S | U | S | H | G | A | G |
| E | N | G | K | O | R | R | L | I | S | L | L |
| G | N | I | B | B | A | T | S | E | R | N | A |

**ALIBIS**

**EVIDENCE**

**FORAGING**

**LIES**

**MILLPOND**

**MURDER**

**POISONING**

**STABBING**

**SUSPECTS**

The six people look up from their pieces of paper, none the wiser. "What does a wordsearch have to do with finding out who committed murder?" Moira mutters under her breath.

The tension in the room is palpable, and Heather brings the sense of theatre to a climax by brandishing one final piece of paper, which she hands a copy of to each of the six. It's almost empty!

"What am I supposed to do with this?" protests Jeremy. "I've had enough of your games, detective! You seem to be treating this like one of those TV detective shows where they gather everyone together at the end to make the big reveal. Well, this is my life you're messing with, so just get on with it and put us out of our misery please!"

"Tough crowd," Heather thinks to herself, before saying out loud: "Indulge me one final time, please. Think like a detective. Transfer anything that it seemed you didn't need from the first grid to this blank one. Then find your names and surnames separately in the new grid of letters you create. I can see you look frazzled, Jeremy, so to spell things out, find your names Gemma, Gus, Moira, Layla, Judith and Jeremy in the grid, and then separately find your surnames Evans, Hawkins, Moore, Baker, Jones and Johnston."

"And then what?" says Jeremy, sweating so much that a big bead of sweat drops from his brow onto the piece of paper in front of him.

"Then," says Heather with a dramatic pause, "you will reveal the killer."

They all audibly gasp, and put their heads down, frantically trying to solve the puzzle. They each complete it at around the same time, then one of them softly says "It's a fair cop" and holds out their hands, ready for the handcuffs to be slapped around their wrists. Who is the murderer?

# EPILOGUE

It was Gus Hawkins, the pillar of the local community and landlord of The Crown! Before Heather escorts him off the premises, she asks why he did it. He replies that he was outraged at the brazen manner in which Dennis and Sam had dismissed his half-sister and her claim to the money. He was in no doubt at all that avarice had got the better of them and they had helped themselves to it. He couldn't let them get away with it. He'd hatched a plan. At first, he just wanted to scare them. When Moira first spoke to them by phone and was rebuffed he'd sent a threatening message to Sam thinking he'd be more likely to crack than Dennis. Heather nods – she'd worked out that the menacing note she'd found in Sam's possessions was actually written by Gus and not Moira. He'd then set up the surprise wine tasting, certain they'd then see sense.

However, when he had read Moira's email explaining the tactic didn't work, he was incandescent with rage. Sam and Dennis were, in truth, just about to leave the pub, and were drunk from all the wine. He'd apologised for springing Moira on them, who they now knew he was related to, and said he'd cook them a slap-up dinner by way of apology, but they'd need to be patient as it would take him a while to rustle it up. They jumped at the chance, particularly when he'd offered them the chance to have a lie down in his private room upstairs to rest up while he cooked their tasty meal.

And so it was that fateful evening he quickly hatched the final, fatal part of his plan. He had overheard enough dull conversations between members of the foraging society over a pint or several to know that fool's funnel would do the job, and that it could plausibly be confused with edible mushrooms. This meant that if he used it to kill two keen members of the foraging society then it would be seen as a case of accidental death or, at worst, another member of the society would be seen as the red-hot suspect, given they would have the expertise to know which mushroom to use.

Things had gone swimmingly – he'd made them both a mushroom risotto, which was on the menu as Heather already knows. This therefore didn't raise any suspicions, and he simply laced it with some fool's funnel. He knew exactly where to find it as he'd seen a fairy ring of the mushrooms growing in a field behind the pub a few days earlier. It was a trivial matter to pop out and get it while the two men slumbered upstairs. They'd both eaten the meal, and washed it down with more wine. They'd then left the pub through the back door so that nobody saw them, very much the worse for wear. He'd arranged for his head barman to drive them home, just telling him that they were drunk: although they lived close enough to the pub to walk home, he didn't want anybody else to see them. Gus was pretty sure he'd given them both a fatal dose and that they'd meet their maker overnight. It'd most likely go down as a case of accidental poisoning and he'd get away with it, he reasoned. He wiped the CCTV footage for the day so that no-one sniffing around would know they were there that evening nor know that they'd spoken to his half-sister earlier in the day. He thought he'd got away with it. And he would have done, if it weren't for that busybody Kevin leading Heather to Moira, which in turn led to the spotlight being turned on him.

Everything matches what Heather had surmised. But what of the stabbing? Gus explains that was a case of needs must. He'd been woken up early in the morning by an angry Dennis Baker knocking at his door sweating and looking as white as a sheet, and demanding to know what Gus had fed him. The landlord quickly calculated that since Dennis lived alone and it was very early, the chances were high that no-one saw him walk to the pub. He could still get away with it, if he acted fast. Dennis either had a strong constitution or, by bad luck, hadn't consumed enough mushrooms to finish him off. He tried to calm him down and, when he wasn't looking, quickly grabbed the first thing he could find – a steak knife, and put it in a bag. He took Dennis for a walk, ostensibly to show him where he'd sourced the mushrooms so Dennis could see they were edible, which was of course a lie.

However, instead he'd taken him near to the secluded millpond and stabbed him through the heart. It was surprisingly easy. He'd then fled back to the pub, knife in hand. He'd thoroughly cleaned the knife, but not before putting on some gloves and dabbing a small amount of blood on some double-sided tape. He knew the knifing muddied the waters with regard to him expecting the police to think both men had been poisoned either accidentally or by a member of the foraging society, but hoped he could still get away with it. Perhaps the police would still think it was a member of the foraging society but that they were trying to double bluff them by also stabbing one of the victims.

He'd then looked for an opportunity to plant the evidence on another suspect. He wanted to find someone with a clear motive to kill Sam, but it was tricky. All he could come up with was Judith, knowing about her past relationship with Sam and recent friction which he'd picked up on through listening in to conversations in the pub. He'd planted some fool's funnel in her bin, and was wondering how to get the police to investigate her when he found out to his delight they already were, although he was concerned when he found out through the grapevine that they only spoke to her briefly.

As for someone connected to Dennis, Gemma was the obvious choice, and so he'd taken the opportunity to give her an innocent hug at the memorial service, and in the process of doing so had quickly taken out the tape and pressed it, and the blood, against her jumper. It was dried by then so he had to hug Gemma quite hard to ensure it rubbed off on her, but luckily she hadn't smelt a rat. He'd tried to get Heather to see the blood by drawing Gemma's jumper to her attention, but frustratingly Heather didn't see it. He was about to be a bit less subtle and point it out directly when Father Stibley came over, and the moment was gone. He'd panicked, nipped away from the service and used a voice-changing app to tip-off the police and suggest they search Judith's bin. Unfortunately she must have had a great alibi, as he was the one being arrested, not her.

Everyone is shocked at his confession. Everyone apart from Heather, that is. She'd worked that all out, and more. She'd worked out the surprising confession given to Father Stibley was by Jeremy, who felt guilty not because he'd committed murder, but simply because he was seeing Dennis's ex-wife and the subterfuge around it. She'd also worked out that Gemma must have known about the money during her marriage to Dennis. When things turned sour, she'd stolen his wedding ring so she could find where it was located, and dug it up and pocketed the money. She'd worn the ring around the house in case the police visited her so that they wouldn't find it, but never wore it outdoors. She'd then been extra nice to Dennis to hopefully prevent him from causing problems if he'd found out what she'd done, whereupon things would inevitably turn messy. This explained the loose soil Heather had seen where Jeremy's blood was found – he'd innocently stumbled there on a later walk; the two of them weren't in cahoots.

Dennis however did check on the bag and realised it was gone. Instead of exacting revenge, he was cognisant Gemma was the mother of his daughter, and so instead cut her out of his will and gave everything to Layla. Heather had found out the date of Dennis's last update to his will was very recent, and therefore he most likely had only just cut Gemma out of the will. Dennis had explained things to Sam, and agreed to pay him £10,000, his share of the money, from his own funds so that his good friend wasn't out of pocket. When Moira had come begging out of the blue demanding her share they'd panicked, and not wanting to give her any of their own money, had decided to simply tell her that someone had stolen the money. They'd hoped that she'd go away quietly. Their actions unfortunately set Gus's evil plan in motion and they walked straight into his lethal trap like a fly unwittingly stumbling into a spider's web.

Gus was given a life sentence, and the pub fell into disuse before being turned into a trendy gastropub some months later. Upper Gorsetown returned to being the ordinary sleepy village it was always meant to be. And as for Heather Vintner and her burgeoning career as a detective of considerable repute? Her story was only just beginning.

# SOLUTIONS

### ① BODY SEARCH

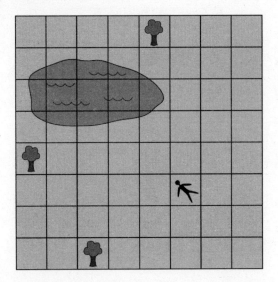

### ② KNIFE CRIME
Answer: HEART.

| P | I | O | U | S |
|---|---|---|---|---|
| C | L | Ǎ | N | K |
| T̷ | R̷ | Ǎ | M | S |
| R̷ | É̌ | Ǎ | L | M |
| H | E | A | R | T |

### ③ SILENT WITNESS
You must combine the two rows of text to create the answer: DENNIS BAKER.

# DENNIS BAKER

## 4  OPEN TO DISPUTE

The society forage for MUSHROOMS.

## 5  HOME VISIT

Sam's house number is 2.

PRESLEY   TURNER   CRUMPET   NEWTON   THATCHER   GILES

## 6  KNOCK, KNOCK

The letter coordinates in the changed squares spell POISONOUS, therefore the mushrooms are not safe to eat.

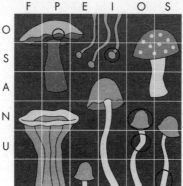

### 7  IS IT ALL AN ACT?
Answer: The pub is called The CROWN.

### 8  LOCAL KNOWLEDGE
The note is a cryptic clue. The word 'somehow' is an anagram indicator, and therefore the letters of 'thickens' must be rearranged to give the eight-letter answer: KITCHENS. Heather must go to the kitchens to find Gus.

### 9  COOKING UP A STORM

THE CROWN

# MENU

**FISH AND CHIPS**

**BANGERS AND MASH**

**LASAGNE**

**MUSHROOM RISOTTO**

**COTTAGE PIE**

# 10 BUILDING BRIDGES

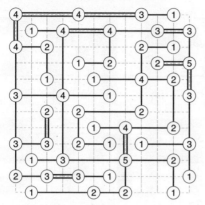

# 11 MUSIC HALL

The person is: JUDITH JONES.

# 12 A SEAT AT THE TABLE

Judith is in seat 4.

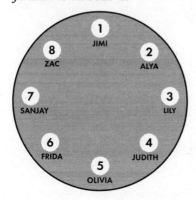

**13** **KEEPING UP WITH THE JONESES**

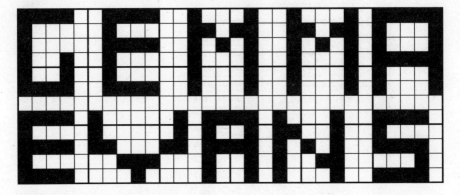

**14** **WHO'S THERE?**

Layla is 18 and her mother Gemma is 36.

**15** **PLAYING GAMES**

The 400th note in the scale is also C. The sequence consists of 14 notes (C,D,E,F,G,A,B,C,B,A,G,F,E,D) before it repeats. 400 / 14 is approximately 28.5, and 28 x 14 = 392. Therefore we know note 392 is at the end of the sequence, D. We therefore count 400 - 392 = 8 places up from the start of the sequence to find the 400th note, which is C.

**16** **YEARS AND YEARS**

Answer: They got divorced six years ago.

## 17 GUT INSTINCT

Answer: RING.

| 57 | 42 | 20 | 82 | 77 | 36 | 31 | 8 | 74 | 67 | 19 | 92 | 86 | 75 | 10 |
|---|---|---|---|---|---|---|---|---|---|---|---|---|---|---|
| 51 | 33 | 58 | 79 | 55 | 21 | 59 | 43 | 88 | 5 | 49 | 59 | 68 | 96 | 92 |
| 33 | 33 | 84 | 15 | 12 | 2 | 64 | 53 | 25 | 80 | 17 | 28 | 77 | 45 | 85 |
| 38 | 28 | 65 | 87 | 10 | 24 | 61 | 69 | 89 | 34 | 66 | 19 | 61 | 52 | 1 |
| 9 | 12 | 42 | 63 | 68 | 91 | 18 | 97 | 85 | 43 | 45 | 31 | 91 | 75 | 92 |
| 93 | 4 | 96 | 44 | 86 | 91 | 94 | 86 | 84 | 83 | 33 | 44 | 75 | 46 | 92 |
| 16 | 82 | 7 | 47 | 87 | 88 | 99 | 75 | 9 | 5 | 92 | 60 | 94 | 95 | 84 |
| 78 | 89 | 60 | 51 | 92 | 34 | 81 | 87 | 11 | 4 | 37 | 99 | 4 | 65 | 21 |
| 79 | 87 | 8 | 58 | 21 | 68 | 6 | 43 | 8 | 90 | 56 | 13 | 68 | 90 | 60 |
| 5 | 88 | 97 | 41 | 73 | 93 | 96 | 54 | 55 | 41 | 4 | 76 | 3 | 20 | 93 |
| 99 | 88 | 95 | 74 | 53 | 89 | 14 | 19 | 66 | 69 | 98 | 44 | 89 | 75 | 80 |
| 13 | 73 | 91 | 49 | 73 | 58 | 69 | 71 | 31 | 43 | 85 | 74 | 36 | 60 | 21 |
| 30 | 39 | 74 | 6 | 74 | 61 | 26 | 72 | 52 | 41 | 40 | 59 | 25 | 35 | 71 |
| 73 | 11 | 78 | 75 | 87 | 13 | 2 | 64 | 29 | 86 | 88 | 70 | 60 | 56 | 20 |
| 44 | 88 | 27 | 89 | 10 | 10 | 22 | 70 | 45 | 92 | 6 | 30 | 90 | 51 | 88 |

## 18 THAT RINGS A BELL

The company is called AlgoFill. To find the answer, count the number of black squares in each grid and convert to a letter using A=1, B=2 and so forth.

## 19 SPLIT DECISION

Swap the first and fifth cards, as shown below, in order to make the equation correct.

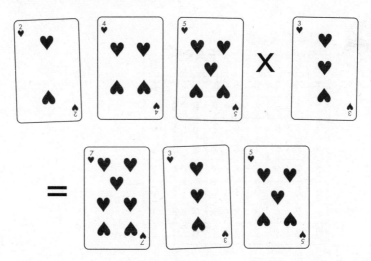

## 20 CAN'T SEE THE WOOD FOR THE TREES

The matching tree is shown below:

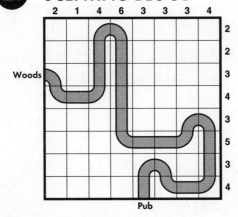

## 21 SCENTING BLOOD

## 22 PUB GRUB

| 8 | 6 | 9 | 7 | 2 | 3 | 4 | 1 | 5 |
|---|---|---|---|---|---|---|---|---|
| 1 | 4 | 3 | 9 | 5 | 8 | 2 | 7 | 6 |
| 2 | 7 | 5 | 6 | 4 | 1 | 8 | 9 | 3 |
| 7 | 1 | 8 | 3 | 9 | 2 | 5 | 6 | 4 |
| 4 | 5 | 6 | 1 | 8 | 7 | 9 | 3 | 2 |
| 3 | 9 | 2 | 4 | 6 | 5 | 1 | 8 | 7 |
| 6 | 8 | 7 | 5 | 1 | 4 | 3 | 2 | 9 |
| 9 | 2 | 4 | 8 | 3 | 6 | 7 | 5 | 1 |
| 5 | 3 | 1 | 2 | 7 | 9 | 6 | 4 | 8 |

## 23 CARELESS WHISPERS

Each letter of the alphabet has been shifted three positions in the code. For instance, 'A' would be represented as 'D' in the code, and so on. The message reads: MEET ME AT THE USUAL LOCATION. SIX THIRTY PM. URGENT.

## 24 THE FINE PRINT

The matching print is E, Jeremy Johnston. A has a shorter line in the middle, B is missing a line at the top, C has a shorter line on the right-middle, D has a shorter line on the bottom-left, and F is missing a line on the right-middle.

## 25 A MAN OF CONVICTION

Jeremy was convicted for DRINK DRIVING, as revealed by the letters in the top and bottom rows of the crossword.

## 26 DNA TEST

What appear to be DNA segments are actually sums. For instance, T-G-C means subtract the values of 'G' and 'C' (using A=1, B=2 etc) from 'T', to create the sum 20 - 7 - 3 = 10 = J, and so on, to spell out the answer: JOHNSTON.

### 27 JOINING THE DOTS

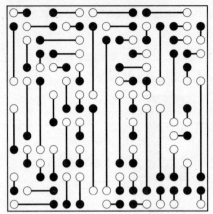

### 28 TAKE NOTE

The recipient of the note was Gemma Evans, whose name the puzzle spells out in Morse code.

### 29 MEETING IN SECRET

Answer: it was three days ago.

### 30 UNDER DISCUSSION

Jeremy wanted to discuss the topic of DIVORCE.

### 31 DIVORCED FROM REALITY

He arranged to meet Gemma at the ALLOTMENT.

### 32 A STING IN THE TAIL

The argument finished at 9:10pm.

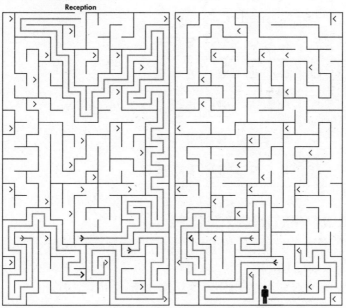

### 33 ENTRY REQUIREMENTS

The answer is 9420.

### 34 HOT DESKING

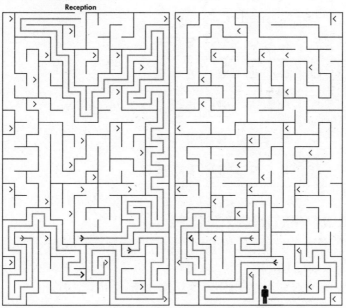

## 35 HUSH, HUSH

The message is in the Pigpen cipher, and reads: THAT MAN WOULD NOT EVEN HURT A FLY.

## 36 WORKER BEE

The letters in numbered squares reveal the answer: NINE PM.

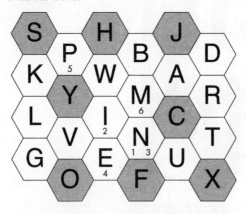

## 37 MOVIE NIGHT

Gemma went to bed at two am in the morning.

| M | A | T | U | R | E |
|---|---|---|---|---|---|
| F | L | O | W | E | R |
| Q | U | E | U | E | S |
| G | O | T | H | I | C |
| C | H | A | N | C | E |
| M | E | D | D | L | E |

## 38 REVERTING TO TYPE

The * symbols indicate keys that were pressed, and how many times. The only word that can be made from the letters C,I,I,O,P,S,S,S,U,U is SUSPICIOUS.

## 39 HISTORY LESSON

Each time consists of two digits. Take the word indicated by the first number, then the letter indicated by the second number. For instance, 42 minutes requires you to take the second letter of the fourth word (the 'T' of 'STARTERS'). Continue in this manner to spell out the word TRUTHFUL. Jeremy is telling the truth.

## 40 THE TRUTH WILL OUT

The shaded squares spell out the name LAYLA.

| | 0 | | | | 4 | | 4 | | |
|---|---|---|---|---|---|---|---|---|---|
| 3 | | | | 8 | | | 7 | 3 | |
| | 0 | | | | | | | | |
| 5 | | | | 7 | | 4 | 4 | | 1 |
| | | 3 | 1 | | | 4 | | | |
| 0 | | 2 | | 0 | | | | | 2 |
| | | 3 | | | 3 | | 5 | | 3 |
| 0 | | | | | | | 5 | | 3 |
| 3 | | 3 | | 0 | | | | | |
| 0 | | 5 | | 1 | 3 | | 5 | 5 | 3 |
| | | | | | | | | 2 | |

## 41 PROFIT MOTIVE

The message reads: THE CAUSE OF DEATH OF DENNIS BAKER HAS BEEN ESTABLISHED AS CONSUMPTION OF POISONOUS MUSHROOMS COMBINED WITH A FATAL INJURY RESULTING FROM BEING STABBED. The code has been created by swapping pairs of letters (and underscores, that represent spaces) around.

## 42 MIND-BLOWING NEWS

The solution words are: jellyfish, frequency, education, situation, important and hurricane. The person Heather is thinking about is: JUDITH.

## 43 IN MEMORIAM

The theme is: FORGIVENESS.

| F | I | R | E | F | I | G | H | T | E | R |
|---|---|---|---|---|---|---|---|---|---|---|
| C | O | M | P | L | I | C | A | T | E | D |
| S | C | R | E | W | D | R | I | V | E | R |
| E | X | A | G | G | E | R | A | T | E | D |
| C | O | N | S | I | D | E | R | A | T | E |
| A | C | H | I | E | V | E | M | E | N | T |
| H | A | I | R | D | R | E | S | S | E | R |
| U | N | F | O | R | T | U | N | A | T | E |
| I | M | M | E | D | I | A | T | E | L | Y |
| P | R | O | T | A | G | O | N | I | S | T |
| M | A | T | H | E | M | A | T | I | C | S |

## 44 SAY IT WITH FLOWERS

Follow the letters of 'FLOWER BOUQUET' repeatedly from start to end to spell out 'GUS' in the grid.

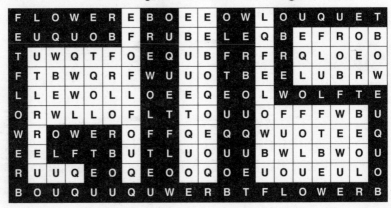

## 45 SECRET CONFESSION

The answers are: sun, felon, nous and fuel. Therefore the name of the mushroom is: FOOL'S FUNNEL.

## 46 NOBODY'S FOOL

At least seven steps are required to solve the puzzle: from square one move to square 6 and then, in turn, 24,22,16,13,31 and 36.

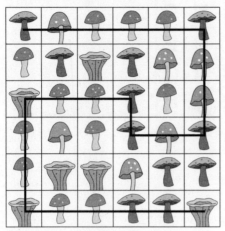

## 47 A GAME OF CHESS

A = rook
B = bishop
C = queen
D = knight
E = king

## 48 A BRIDGE TOO FAR

| 2♠ | 4♦ | 5NT | 3♥ | A♣ |
|---|---|---|---|---|
| 5♥ | 3♣ | A♠ | 2♦ | 4NT |
| 4♣ | 5♠ | 3♦ | A NT | 2♥ |
| A♦ | 2NT | 4♥ | 5♣ | 3♠ |
| 3NT | A♥ | 2♣ | 4♠ | 5♦ |

**49** **MIXED SUCCESS**

Judith's partner is called CONNOR.

| C | N | R | O | E | T |
|---|---|---|---|---|---|
| T | O | E | R | N | C |
| O | R | N | T | C | E |
| E | T | C | N | R | O |
| R | E | T | C | O | N |
| N | C | O | E | T | R |

**50** **TIMES TABLE**

CONNOR appears five times:

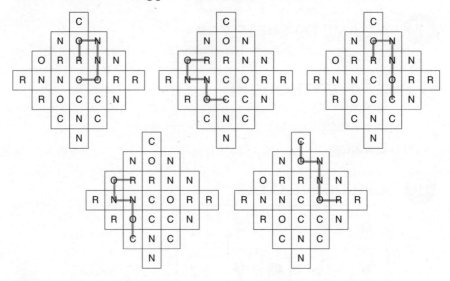

**51** **SILENT PARTNER**

The restaurant's name is spelled out using Braille characters. Working clockwise around the words 'DINNER RECEIPT', starting above the 'D' of 'dinner', the restaurant name is revealed as THE ENCHANTED GARDEN RESTAURANT.

## 52 HOME, SWEET HOME

The quickest route that starts at Ivyville, ends at Pebbleston, and visits each other location once along the way is 67 miles long. The route is: Ivyville, Willowbrook, Oakvale, Cedardale, Fernwood and then, finally, Pebbleston.

## 53 NIGHT TRAIN

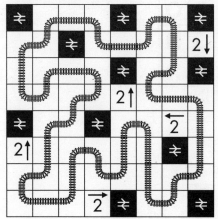

## 54 TRAIN OF THOUGHT

The eight-letter word Heather created is: PHYSICAL.

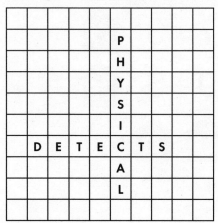

## 55 DEAR DIARY

The correct order is 19, 2, 20, 25, 0, 11 to create the apposite password: LOCKED.

## 56 ON SCHEDULE

The code works by adding a nonsense letter after each letter of the message, which must be ignored, for instance: TOEZNS represents 'TEN'. The message reads:

TEN AM PLANT RASPBERRY CANES AT THE ALLOTMENT

TWELVE PM CALL WITH CAROL ABOUT FORAGING SOCIETY ELECTIONS THEN GO TO WOODS AND PICK MUSHROOMS FOR LUNCH

TWO PM LUNCH THEN MEET DENNIS AT PUB FOR WINE TASTING

## 57 GRUDGE MATCH

Mo's house is number 14.

| | | | | |
|---|---|---|---|---|
| *3 | 6 | 8 | 9 | 26 |
| *1 | 2 | 3 | 4 | 10 |
| 2 | 5 | 7 | *3 | 17 |
| 8 | *7 | 9 | 5 | 29 |
| 14 | 20 | 27 | 21 | |

## 58 PRINT PREVIEW

Where a hole is present at the start of a line of text on the printout you should take the first letter from that line to create the message: KEEP HER SWEET.

## 59 LOCATION, LOCATION, LOCATION

You must read down column one, then up column two, down column three and so on to reveal the message: LOCATION IS ROW THREE COLUMN NINE.

## 60 SAFE CODE

The first four buttons pressed are shown here:

| 2↓ | 2↓ | 2← | 3↓ | 3↓ |
|---|---|---|---|---|
| 1→ | X | 2/3↓ | 1→ | 3↓ |
| 1↓ | 3→ | 2↑ | 1↑ | 2← |
| 3↗ | 4/3↑ | 1/2↑ | 1↑ | 1↙ |
| 3↑ | 1← | 3/1↖ | 2← | 4↑ |

## 61 POISON PEN LETTER

There is only one way to select one letter from each row to create a word, which is: REVENGE.

## 62 IN THE MONEY

The code works as follows: 'V' stands for 'vowel' and 'C' for 'consonant'. V1 is the first vowel, which is 'A' whilst V5 is the final vowel, which is 'U'. C1 is the first consonant which is 'B', whilst C21 is the final consonant, which is 'Z'. This reveals the following:

| Date | Amount (£) | Credit/debit | Details |
|---|---|---|---|
| Xx/xx/xxxx | 5.00 | CREDIT | INTEREST |
| Xx/xx/xxxx | 1,100 | DEBIT | MORTGAGE PAYMENT |
| Xx/xx/xxxx | 10,000 | CREDIT | FROM DENNIS BAKER |

The surprising element is that Dennis Baker recently transferred Sam the sizeable sum of £10,000.

**63** **THREATENING BEHAVIOUR**

Each word has an additional letter added. Remove the letter referenced for each word underneath the text. For instance, remove the third letter of 'WHEY' to create the word 'WHY'. The note reads: WHY NOW? NO GOOD CAN COME OF THIS.

**64** **FOOD FOR THOUGHT**

Heather bought one bag of crisps, three chocolate bars and two drinks.

**65** **A SHAKY START**

Moira drank 100ml on her first gulp, leaving 200ml. She drank half on her second gulp, leaving 100ml. 70% of that is 70ml, therefore there is 30ml left in the glass.

**66** **IDENTITY CRISIS**

A's nose is upside down, B's beauty mark is on the opposite cheek, C has no eyebrows, and E's forehead is higher. Therefore the answer is D.

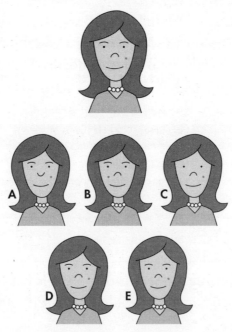

## INNOCENT PARTY

Moira is a DOCTOR.

| S | A | I | D |
|---|---|---|---|
| A | C | R | E |
| I | R | O | N |
| D | E | N | T |

## THE GRAVEYARD SHIFT

The answers are: BRUSCHETTA (an anagram of 'at butcher's'), ROOSEVELT (an anagram of 'sole voter'), PARDON (par + don), THINKING (thin + king), APRICOT (concealed in 'cheap ricotta') and YETI (yet + i). The hospital name is: COUNTY GENERAL.

## A CHANGE OF DIRECTION

The letters 'A' and 'I' have been swapped around, and likewise the letters 'E' and 'O'. Switching them back creates the following:

**OBSTETRICS**
FIRST FLOOR, GREEN ZONE
**CRITICAL CARE**
SECOND FLOOR, RED ZONE
**HAEMATOLOGY**
THIRD FLOOR, YELLOW ZONE
**DIETETICS**
SECOND FLOOR, GREEN ZONE
**NEPHROLOGY**
FIRST FLOOR, YELLOW ZONE
**CARDIOLOGY**
THIRD FLOOR, GREEN ZONE
**NEONATAL**
SECOND FLOOR, YELLOW ZONE.

Therefore Heather needs to go to DIETETICS, on the second floor.

**HOSPITAL PASS**

Moira did indeed work from 6pm to 6am so she is telling the truth.

| Employee | Hours worked | Room Number | Supervisor |
|----------|--------------|-------------|------------|
| Dominic | 4pm-4am | 3 | Dr. Ramirez |
| Isabella | 5pm-5am | 1 | Dr. Hawthorne |
| Janice | 3pm-3am | 2 | Dr. Chen |
| Moira | 6pm-6am | 4 | Dr. Nguyen |

 **DEAD END**

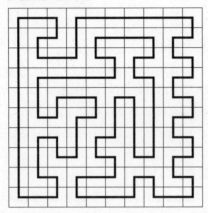

 **THREE'S A CROWD**

Answer: ROYALTY.

**PUB FENG SHUI**

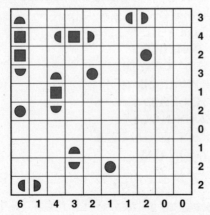

## 74 TABLE TALK

The numberplate is: GF31 EFG.

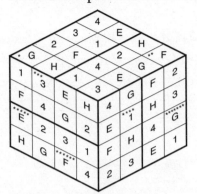

## 75 PLATE RECOGNITION

The owner of the car is: MOIRA MOORE.

## 76 LAW OF AVERAGES

Sam and Moira's combined height is 328cm, since the total height of the three is 167x3 = 501cm, from which we subtract Dennis's height.

We know that Moira cannot be the tallest as we are told she is shorter than Sam. If we consider the case where Sam is the tallest of the three, then he must be taller than 173cm. If he were 174cm tall, that would make Moira 154cm tall, which is a spread of 20 centimetres. Therefore Sam cannot be the tallest.

This means Dennis is the tallest. One of the other two is therefore 158cm tall and the other is 170cm tall. Since we know Moira is shorter than Sam she must be 158cm, and Sam is 170cm tall.

**77 RINGING A BELL**

The answer, appropriately, is: FORGETFUL.

**78 LACK OF CONVICTION**

The distances are: Bramblewood: 7 miles, Brackenwood: 4 miles, Briarwood: 6 miles. Therefore Heather should go to BRAMBLEWOOD.

**79 IN THE WEEDS**

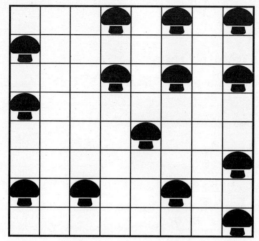

**80 TAKE FIVE**

| 2 | 1 | 4 | 6 | 9 | 3 | 8 | 7 | 5 |
|---|---|---|---|---|---|---|---|---|
| 3 | 5 | 9 | 7 | 8 | 1 | 2 | 4 | 6 |
| 6 | 7 | 8 | 4 | 5 | 2 | 9 | 1 | 3 |
| 1 | 2 | 6 | 9 | 3 | 5 | 7 | 8 | 4 |
| 5 | 9 | 7 | 8 | 6 | 4 | 1 | 3 | 2 |
| 8 | 4 | 3 | 2 | 1 | 7 | 6 | 5 | 9 |
| 4 | 3 | 2 | 1 | 7 | 9 | 5 | 6 | 8 |
| 9 | 8 | 1 | 5 | 4 | 6 | 3 | 2 | 7 |
| 7 | 6 | 5 | 3 | 2 | 8 | 4 | 9 | 1 |

**81** **SHOW ME THE MONEY**

They decided to bury it for 20 years.

**82** **HARD TIMES**

Each vowel has been shifted back to the previous vowel (e.g. 'I' is represented as 'E' in the code, 'E' is represented by 'A' in the code), and likewise each consonant has been shifted back to the previous consonant (e.g. 'M' is represented by 'L' in the code, 'F' is represented by 'D' in the code). The message reads: Imagine my surprise when I found loose earth, dug it up, and found that there was nothing there but the empty bag! Not only had they clearly taken the money for themselves, I'd wager they did it fairly recently too.

**83** **LADY LUCK**

Words that can be made include: ABLE, AMBLE, AMBLING, BABE, BAD, BADE, BAG, BAGEL, BAP, BAUBLE, BEG, BELIE, BLUE, BULB, GABLE, GAMBLE and MAMBA. The longest word, and therefore the source of Moira's debts, is GAMBLING.

## 84 YOUR NUMBER'S UP

The phone number is: 17938 423671.

| 2 | 7 | 5 | 4 | 6 | 8 | 9 | 3 | *1 |
|---|---|---|---|---|---|---|---|---|
| 3 | 1 | 4 | *7 | 5 | 9 | 2 | 6 | 8 |
| *9 | 6 | 8 | 1 | 2 | 3 | 7 | 4 | 5 |
| 5 | 2 | 9 | *3 | 4 | 7 | 1 | *8 | 6 |
| 7 | *4 | 6 | 5 | 8 | 1 | 3 | 9 | *2 |
| 8 | *3 | 1 | *6 | 9 | 2 | 4 | 5 | 7 |
| 1 | 9 | *7 | 8 | 3 | 5 | 6 | 2 | 4 |
| 6 | 8 | 2 | 9 | 7 | 4 | 5 | *1 | 3 |
| 4 | 5 | 3 | 2 | 1 | 6 | 8 | 7 | 9 |

## 85 WHAT HAPPENED NEXT?

The only word that can be made, and how Moira felt, is: FOILED.

## 86 SURPRISE, SURPRISE

The longest word that can be made is: CHAMPAGNE.

## 87 DIGGING UP THE PAST

A has a line missing at the top, one of the lines in the middle of C has moved, the bottom-left bulge of D is smaller, the top-right bulge of E is larger, and F has a smaller hole, therefore the answer is B.

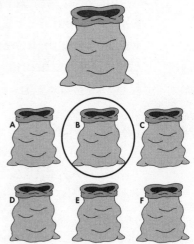

**REVENGE IS A DISH BEST SERVED COLD**

Each letter has been shifted 13 places in the alphabet, therefore 'A' is represented by 'N', whilst 'N' is represented by 'A', and so on. The message reads: THEY FINALLY ADMITTED THAT THEY HAD DUG UP THE BAG BUT INSISTED THAT WHEN THEY DID SO IT WAS EMPTY. I DON'T BELIEVE A WORD THAT THEY SAY, OF COURSE. CLEARLY THEY'VE HELPED THEMSELVES TO THE MONEY. I CAN'T GO TO THE POLICE BUT I CAN'T LET THIS REST. I'LL HAVE A THINK ABOUT IT FOR A WHILE AND WORK OUT HOW TO PROCEED.

**CAUGHT ON CAMERA**

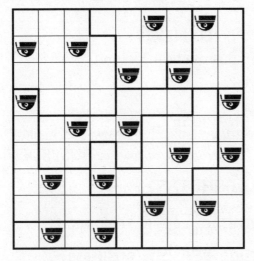

 **RING BEARER**

There are 26 red cards in a pack of 52 cards. The first card therefore has a 26/52 chance of being red, the second card has a 25/51 chance and the third card has a 24/50 chance. Multiply these fractions together to get 15,600/132,600 which reduces to a 2/17 or approximately 11.76% chance of Gemma telling the truth.

## 91 A SPOT OF BOTHER

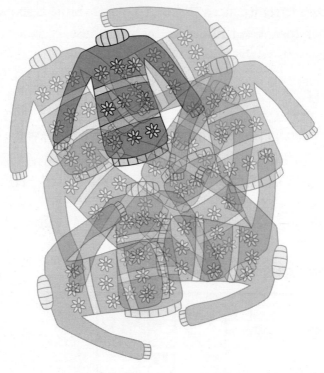

## 92 PUB LUNCH

The linking words are box, club, show, eye, bank, flow, land and key. Therefore the answer is: BUSYBODY.

SOAP **B** O **X** OFFICE

NIGHT C L **U B** SANDWICH

SLIDE **S** H O **W** BUSINESS

PRIVATE E **Y** E WITNESS

PIGGY **B** A N **K** HOLIDAY

CASH F L **O** W CHART

CRASH L A N **D** LINE

SKELETON **K** E **Y** SIGNATURE

### 93 MONEY TALKS

The letters P, I, C, S, F, I and T combine with the 'A' to create the word PACIFIST, which is how Gus described himself.

# PACIFIST

### 94 PRESSURE COOKER

# ASPARAGUS
# ONION
# SPINACH

### 95 SAFE HAVEN

The code for the safe is: 8607.

## 96 HIGH STAKES

The DNA matches with sample C.

| A | T | C | C | A | A | A | A | A | T |
|---|---|---|---|---|---|---|---|---|---|
| A | C | A | T | T | C | T | C | T | A |
| C | A | A | C | G | C | A | C | C | C |
| C | T | A | A | C | A | C | C | C | G |
| A | C | A | T | G | A | T | G | G | C |
| T | T | T | T | A | C | C | A | A | A |
| A | T | C | T | G | C | A | C | C | A |
| C | G | C | A | T | C | G | C | T | G |
| C | T | G | A | C | G | A | C | A | A |
| G | C | A | T | A | C | T | A | C | G |

## 97 A SPANNER IN THE WORKS

## 98 WHODUNIT?

The puzzle solves, so Heather is right – she knows who has committed murder.

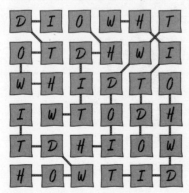

**LAST ORDERS**

The solution is: 1) Gemma 2) Gus 3) Moira 4) Layla 5) Judith 6) Jeremy. The people who start sweating are therefore Gemma and Jeremy.

 **MURDER WILL OUT**

This is the solution to the first puzzle. Take the first letter from the person at table one, the second from the person at table two and so on to spell out the word GUILTY.

| 1 | G | E | M | M | A | |
| 2 | G | U | S | | | |
| 3 | M | O | I | R | A | |
| 4 | L | A | Y | L | A | |
| 5 | J | U | D | I | T | H |
| 6 | J | E | R | E | M | Y |

This is the solution to the larger wordsearch:

The unused letters (highlighted in grey above) should now be transferred to the blank 9x9 grid to create a new wordsearch.

Once solved, the remaining letters in the grid reveal that GUS HAWKINS IS THE KILLER.

## PIGPEN CIPHER

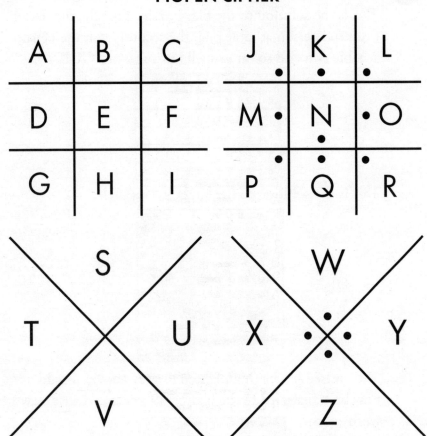

# MORSE CODE

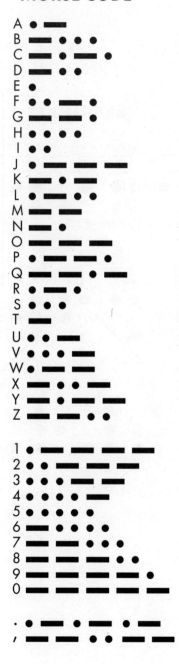

## BRAILLE KEY

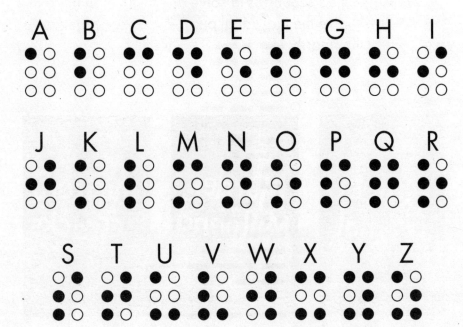

# COSY CRIME PUZZLES

Put your detective hat on, use all your powers of logic and deduction to tackle these 100 original murder-mystery puzzles. Gather the clues and summon all your super-sleuthing skills to solve this super-fiendish and addictive murder-mystery case file.

100 crime-related scenarios to solve as you take on the role of detective. Solve the individual puzzles to piece together what led to the ghastly events.

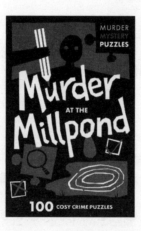

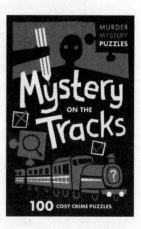

**Killer on the Canal**

ISBN: 978-0-00-871005-7

Pub Date: 18th July 2024

**Murder at the Millpond**

ISBN: 978-0-00-871007-1

Pub Date: 12th September 2024

**Mystery on the Tracks**

ISBN: 978-0-00-871006-4

Pub Date: 7th November 2024

# Puzzle it out with Collins

**Killer on the Canal**
ISBN 978-0-00-871005-7
Pub date 18th July 2024

After his best friend Fred is murdered, narrowboat enthusiast Harvey Rivers finds himself caught up in a deadly conspiracy. Follow Harvey as he chases Fred's killer across the length of the country, meeting eccentric characters and facing unusual challenges on the way. With his loyal dog, Pembroke, he's more than a match for anything the canals can throw at him.

# Puzzle it out with Collins

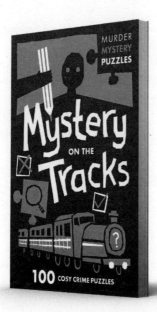

**Mystery on the Tracks**
ISBN 978-0-00-866072-7
Pub date 7th November 2024

Meet Adrienne Sandford, police detective and art connoisseur. After years toiling away in London, she considers herself lucky for finally finding the time to take a train to Italy – until another passenger is found stabbed to death in their cabin, that is. As the train crosses the Alps and murders multiply, Adrienne must apply all her wits to make it safely to Rome.

# Puzzle it out with Collins

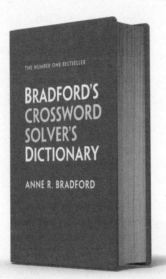

**Bradford's Crossword Solver's Dictionary**
ISBN 978-0-00-867303-1
Pub date 12th September 2024

The bestselling companion for all crossword solvers and compilers. Compiled over 60 years by a single author based on her experience of solving crosswords each day, this companion is regarded by top compilers as the authority for solvers and setters alike. Anne Bradford's work is now continued by her daughter Gillian.

Every word has appeared as a solution to a real crossword clue making it the must-have crossword dictionary for all cryptic and quick crosswords lovers.

# Puzzle it out with Collins

**Collins Pub Quiz**
ISBN 978-0-00-867308-6
Pub date 12th September 2024

500 brand new, up-to-date quizzes and 10,000 questions covering topics from pop stars to death stars, choose your rounds from general knowledge, specialist subjects and pot luck with questions from teasers to terrors that will scramble even an egghead's brains.

Designed to be played on your own or with family and friends, the man down the road and two halves of the crowd at your local. Each quiz provides good clean fun for all.

The answers are quick and easy to find so that anyone can pick this up and become a top quiz master.

# Puzzle it out with Scrabble™

### Official Scrabble™ Words
ISBN 978-0-00-866072-7
Pub date 15th August 2024

**The ultimate Scrabble bible!**
With more than 280,000 permissible words, including inflected forms, this is the ideal training and adjudication tool for everyone playing Scrabble. Endorsed by Mattel and WESPA (the World English-Language Scrabble Players Association) this is the essential reference for all Scrabble players.

### Scrabble™ Dictionary
ISBN 978-0-00-866073-4
Pub date 29th August 2024

Not sure if a word is valid in Scrabble play? Collins SCRABBLE™ Dictionary is fully updated to include all valid words between 2 and 9 letters in length from the latest official Scrabble word list, making it a must-have to settle disputes over eligible words.

# Puzzle it out with Scrabble™

### Scrabble™ Puzzles Book 2
**ISBN 978-0-00-866076-5**
**Pub date 29th August 2024**

The ideal gift for all word puzzle enthusiasts! 250 fun puzzles for word game lovers. Based on techniques required for Scrabble, these challenges have been designed to put your word power to the ultimate test. All words used are from the official Scrabble word list, so you learn as you play.
Suitable for the whole family.

### Scrabble™ Secrets
**ISBN 978-0-00-859123-6**
**Pub date 12th September 2024**

- Tips and tricks that are perfect for Scrabble enthusiasts at any level with fun and easy ways to memorise words
- Find out how to handle a rack full of vowels or consonants
- Contains a full list of playable 2 and 3 letter words

# Puzzle it out with *The Times*

### The Times Kakuro Book 1
**ISBN 978-0-00-867306-2**
**Pub date 29th August 2024**

200 mathematical and logic puzzles to test your mental dexterity with this collection from the The Times. Just like a mathematical crossword. Ideal for all fans of Su Doku who relish grappling with figures.

### The Times Polygon Book 1
**ISBN 978-0-00-866073-4**
**Pub date 29th August 2024**

300 word puzzles to test your mental dexterity with this collection from The Times. The perfect challenge for all lovers of wordsearch and crosswords.

# Puzzle it out with *The Times*

### The Times Jumbo Cryptic Crossword Book 23
**ISBN 978-0-00-867312-3**
**Pub date 29th August 2024**

This supremely challenging cryptic collection contains 50 jumbo-sized, large grid puzzles, conceived to really challenge your word skills.

### The Times Samurai Su Doku Book 13
**ISBN 978-0-00-867313-0**
**Pub date 15th August 2024**

For anyone who loves the challenge of Su Doku but manages to solve them within minutes, you can now enjoy the extended mental workout and ultimate endurance test of a five grid interlinked system.

# Puzzle it out with *The Sunday Times*

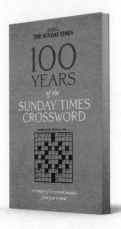

### 100 Years of the Sunday Times Crossword
**ISBN 978-0-00-867309-3**
**Pub date 12th September 2024**

The Sunday Times Crossword will be 100 years old in 2025. It is the oldest of the broadsheet newspaper crosswords which are now cryptic. Discover how the puzzles have developed over the years in this celebration of a century of crosswords, from 1925, when the first one was printed in The Sunday Times, to today.

### The Sunday Times Cryptic Crossword Book 4
**ISBN 978-0-00-867311-6**
**Pub date 29th August 2024**

A compilation of 100 cryptic crosswords from The Sunday Times, one of the greatest crossword puzzle challenges. These brainteasers will test all cryptic crossword lovers to the limit!